"QUOTE ME"
THE BOOK OF ALL
NEW QUOTES

BY

JOSEPH JULIUS BONKOWSKI JR.

Copyright © 2009 by Joseph Julius Bonkowski Jr.

"Quote Me" The Book Of All New Quotes
by Joseph Julius Bonkowski Jr.

Printed in the United States of America

ISBN 978-1-60791-990-2

All rights reserved solely by the author. The author guarantees all contents are original and do not infringe upon the legal rights of any other person or work. No part of this book may be reproduced in any form without the permission of the author. The views expressed in this book are not necessarily those of the publisher.

Edited by Dorothy R Bonkowski

www.xulonpress.com

INTRODUCTION
All quotes or sayings in this book are by Joseph Bonkowski and are all new!!!

A short saying or quote is nothing but philosophy. In short philosophy is the love and pursuit of wisdom, by word of mouth or written down, using some form of reality, knowledge, logic, reasoning, analysis, beliefs, conception, teaching, all or some of these are summed up in a short phrase or two. Basically anything used to make you think, usually cleverly written, and usually in a different view point from the normal.

To coin a phrase "Modern philosophy" This is a new type of philosophy, designed for today's times, written with technology use in them like cell phones, computers, T.V. radio, video, etc... it's basically anything post W.W.I.

Some philosophy is complex, and many people won't read it, but they do like simply philosophy, this is what I call bumper sticker philosophy, I think it's just more fun to read and what most of this book is. Basically slow read and enjoy, a bathroom book that you can pick up or put down at you're convince. The modest author wishes you, the reader will derive many a chuckle and much enjoyment from the truisms contained in this thought provoking work.

If you are a socialist and want to skip the socialist chapter fine, but everything in this book the author considers good reading. There are about 4,500 quotes in this book.

THIS BOOK IS A COLLECTION OF NEW SHORT SAYINGS AND QUOTES.

Acknowledgments

GOD!

TABLE OF CONTENTS.

Disclaimer,

No one has read everything ever written including the author, billions of stories, books, sayings, scripts, newspapers etc... that have been written, by authors, famous people and common people. When writing several thousand sayings or quotes some are bound to already have been written unbeknown to the author, many are outright copied first or last part of a famous quote, but rewritten, due to space and not knowing who wrote many of the famous quotes the original author is not mentioned, but a word or two was changed or more added or taken away that would make it a NEW SAYING or a NEW QUOTE.

NOTICE: The majority of this book is simply written and cleverly written, with a few humorous puns, this book was written in a slightly Christian conservative view point, but that is only some of the quotes, this book was written to entertain and make you think, to make you appreciate good humor and well written sayings. This book should give you several hours of entertainment and many quotes have double means, and some are so cleverly written you may have to re-read anything that doesn't make sense the first time you read it. This book was not meant to put any race, sex, religion, person or people down, it is not intended as a personal attack on anyone or any people, some sayings are satire or a parody, but the author does need something to write about or there would be no book, this book is intended to entertain you, and to help you, help you to quit procrastination, stop a bad habit, get out of debt, or just to get your mind off your worries.

To order a copy of this book go to <u>www.xulonpress.com</u> or ask your local bookstore.

*ABORTION*ANYONE FEEL FREE TO USE ANY ABORTION QUOTE.
(Written by Joseph Bonkowski)

Does abortion mean that God made a mistake??

Abortion is the war against children.

Millions go to amusement parks each day, and only a few on an abortion protest line.

Abortion, you vote yes, the baby votes no, we have a tie, we need a tie breaker, ask your mother.

Abortion- Thou shall not kill.

To the abortionist, I say your mother didn't believe in abortion.

Liquor helps makes the baby, abortion kills the baby.

"Kill the baby" quoted the liberal.

Abortion is an accident waiting to happen.

Abortion is legal because babies can't vote.

Man has figured out when life has started, so he created the condom.

Life begins at conception and ends with just one word, heaven or hell?

If your mother believed in abortion you would not be here.

Paradox- Prolife.

I am outnumbered a million for abortion, and only one against, two against counting GOD.

Suicide is a choice, abortion isn't.

They call abortion choice, so then give me the choice to vote on it.

Less abort abortion.

What if Jesus had been aborted?

There were only 3,000 dead in 911 in only one day, and it's big news, and 20,000 per day die from abortion everyday and it's not news!?

The Supreme Court voted to make abortion legal, one day God will vote the Supreme Court to go to hell.

ALCOHOL************************
(Written by Joseph Bonkowski)

Booze takes the edge off, but will drive you over the edge.

Gin is in,
Wine is fine,
Beer with a cheer,
Our last hour is upon us,
Last call, last call.

I drink and drive because the state store is too far to walk.

A shot of liquor can bring out a gun shot. (Three meanings for this)

Exercise is a beer and the couch for me.

A genie in a bottle is not 100 proof.

The glass is only empty when your wallet is empty.

If you kill a fifth of liquor every day, one day the fifth will kill you.

Even a drunk has the right of the fifth.

Children cry and adults drink.

Sobriety, I'll drink to that.

I'm never tardy to the party.

Two men had a dream, one man said I'll drink to that, and the other man lived his dreams.

Drinking doesn't interfere with my depression, the bar tab does.

My rum is my old friend,
My old friend that makes me dumb,
But I have fun with my rum.

The cares of the day can be washed away with the booze of the night.

The boozer thinks the loser is the one sitting next to him at the bar.

Cheers, to the end of my alcoholism.

I hate to drink alone, so I get my ice drunk.

Spilt wine can be sour grapes.

Liquor makes you a boozer loser.

No gin, no sin.

I'm not going to the bar; I'm going to the pub.

Think don't drink.

To those who are a member of A.A. and A.A.A. don't drink and drive.

I exercise my arm and liver at the sports bar.

Cheer up and drink up, cheers.

When gin turns to sin, you will need bail for jail.

From drink to drunk,
It's not very far to the bar,
I drink until I stink,
I think I need another drink.

Friendship in a bar won't go very far.

A fifth of alcohol brings out the Fifth Amendment.

I'm not lonely I have a beer for company.

Wine brings the truth out.

In heaven there is no beer, but we do have communion wine here.

Beer in and belly out.

To drink clouds up the memory and it looks like cloudy days ahead.

I don't think wine will make you divine.

Reasonable argument, don't drink to that.

A drink to help me over my crisis and it's over, another drink and it becomes a crisis.

Wine makes the fool out of the wise.

Closing time, the bartender hates to lose the money and likes to lose the drunks.

I don't drink and drive, even if someone drives me to drink.

ANIMAL*************************
(Written by Joseph Bonkowski)

The fish eats first and you might eat second says the fisherman.

A mouse can make an elephant run, a cat can make a mouse run, and an elephant can make a cat run.

The mouse that thinks he's a lion will soon be eaten by a cat.

Animal kill's animal that's life, man is an animal that's life, and a man that kills man does life.

Chickens are chicken to fly.

A wallaby is want to be kangaroo.

Why did the chicken cross the road? He didn't want to have all his eggs in one basket.

When the cats away then beware of the dog.

The straw that broke the camel's back weighs no more than the other straws.

Too many pets spoil the yard.

Two on a horse slows the horse.

I went skeet shooting, and Peta stopped me.

I have termites so now I need some carpenter ants.

A bug was bugging me, so I sprayed it to bug the bug.

Where the trees be the birds be,
Where the trees be bumblebee's be,
Where the trees be the lumberjack be.

God knows what he is doing; an elephants has big ears so he can hear you talking about his weight problem.

Only the fish that opens his mouth gets in trouble.

Sometimes the fish is the meal, and sometimes the fish gets the meal.

A small man is like a small dog, always barking about what he can do.

A fried chicken lays no eggs.

Dogs are made in heaven, and dog collars in China.

Bee bee flee from me, if not I will flee from thee.

Bee VS Bear,
The bear was in the air,
Up in a tree with a bee,
And the bee on his behind,
It's all just a story,
It's like the tortoise and the hare,
But this one was in the air.

The parrot is the master of gossip, but still he only repeats what he hears.

The fly told himself that he could fly, he also told the caterpillar.

When a fish says food, you have food. Quote the fisherman.

If you don't train your dog your dog will train you.

Which came first the chicken or the egg? The chicken, see Genesis 1-21.

You can lead a horse to water, but you can't get him drunk.

He's nosier than a blood hound.

The chicken that doesn't lay eggs becomes fried chicken.

A bird flies away from trouble, a birdbrain towards trouble.

From a mouse to a lion is the kid with a big dog.

Water under the bridge, do you thinks there's fish in that water?

One day the lamb decided to lie down with the lion, that day the lion ate lamb chops.

A bird thinks a worm is valuable and not gold, what a bird brain.

There's a chicken in every pot if you are lucky, if not its pot luck.

I washed my hair and my hare caught a cold.

If you count your chickens before the hatch, you might only have eggs.

If it looks like a duck, quacks like a duck, then I suggest you better duck.

Hungry fish, full me.

The fox is in the hen house, and we keep re-electing the fox.

A mouse sees a cat differently than I do.

All caterpillars imagine they are butterflies.

Be like the bear that does his business in the woods, and keep your business to yourself.

I used to hate poodles until one owned me.

Alligator in the water,
I say "See you later alligator,"
Alligator on land,
I say "See you later alligator,"
Alligator by my car,
I say "luggage."

The one winged bird can't fly in a circle but can fry in a pan.

I was in a spelling bee, the prize was honey.

Be like a bear that does his business in the woods, and keep your business to yourself, I can't believe someone wrote this crap.

Fear a big dog, but watch for a small dog.

Your dog and your mother both think you are swell, and if you think this you have a swelled head.

The horse I have at home doesn't eat, its worse, it takes gasoline.

It's mostly the blind that notice the birds.

A mouse can move an elephant.

Don't feed the cat if there's a mouse in the house.

Eggs aren't why the fox wants in the hen house.

The swiftest horse still needs directions.

Oh the joy to play with a dog,
Oh the fear of being bitten.

Exterminators bug me.

A man that puts a squirrel in his pants is nuts.

There is no use in beating a dead horse, for the horse has learned its lesson.

The straw that broke the camel's back need not be a straw.

Take a gander at the gander for his goose will soon be cooked.

Which came first the fried chicken or the fried eggs?

The chicken doesn't care where the seeds come from that he eats, and I don't care where the chicken comes from that I eat.

You can lead a horse to water and then get in your car and go.

The ants, the bees, and the employed are a form of slavery, I won't rest until I free the ants and the bees.

You don't see two ants fighting, but you do two elephants.

My rights are like a caterpillar, for they can change into a butterfly and fly away.

If the mule was a mute I could see him being so stubborn.

You can't get an egg from a fried chicken, but you can get fried chicken from an egg, you just have to wait.

Do not enter, so we must try to find another way around, I think that's why the chicken crossed the road.

Meat is murder, and I like my murder well done.

Life is like a butterfly, when we think life is going one way, it changes, and your dreams fly out the window.

Man is the only animal that cages other animals, including himself.

Does day follow night or night follow day says the chicken to the egg?

Give a man a fish and you may have to also teach him how to cook it.

The snake knows not that he ate your pet, and neither does he know when he is your pet.

The chicken that stops laying eggs becomes fried chicken.

The tortoise and the hare race, the hare wins by a hair.

Birds only sing when you open your ears.

Every dog has his day,
Adopt a pet today.

The early bird still has time to crap on your car.

The devil would make a good dog, I never have to call him and he's always there.

A mouse with the heart of a lion will soon be eaten by a cat.

Why did the chicken cross the road? To sell eggs.

Why did the chicken cross the road? To escape from K.F.C.

Hesitation cost the cat the rat.

In good times we get a bone for the dog, in bad times we get a bone for the dog.

In good times we get a bone for the dog, in bad times we get a bone for the dog, lucky dog.

In good times we get a bone for the dog, and in bad times we get a bone for ourselves.

In good times we get a bone for the dog, in bad times we get rid of the dog.

No use crying over spilt milk just let the cat in.

The biggest difference I can see between a lion and a lamb is we eat lamb.

The grass is always greener on the other side, but when you get to the other side you find the dog has left you his calling card, and maybe that's why the grass is greener?

Small bites can eat an elephant.

A dog and a frog where sitting on a log, the dog says what's the meaning of life, and the frog says ribbitt.

The buck stops here; said the hunter.

The fly is useless, and the horse is not, so the fly tries to be a horse by hanging onto the horse, but only becomes a horsefly.

In fishing or politics lies are expected.

The obscure make a mouse move an elephant.

Can a bird fly if he thinks he can't?

Did you hear about the tortoise and the hare? The tortoise shaved and the hair was no more.

A trillion fish in the sea and none on the line, and when I leave I will be the one that got away.

Most people don't hear birds in the city.

An alternative thought is made after you see the size of the dog.

If a cat has a split personality, does each have 4 ½ life's?

A lion needs no eyes to smell fear, and I need no eyes to fear a lion.

Listen to the birds, they are happy singing their songs, yet they have no money, can't we learn from them?

I smell a rat, it turns out it was just Chinese food.

Hang a horse thief, and probation for a car thief, my how times have changed.

Lions like lamb chops and must be a lion to get them.

The little piggy that went wee wee wee all of the way home should have used the bathroom before leaving home.

The fatter the cat the bigger the rats.

A fine bird makes a fine pillow; a fowl bird makes a fine meal.

Why did the chicken cross the road, to buy eggs.

If you don't plan for a chicken in your pot, you won't have a pot to plan in.

A good friend will try to love you more than your dog.

The tortoise and the hare race, a bear eats the hare and the tortoise says to the bear "I told you he would be there."

****ART**************************************
(Written by Joseph Bonkowski)

From junk to genius is art.

Art- if the price is high it's underpriced.

Art, The more it cost the better it looks.

No painting on canvas is perfection until the price hits a million dollars.

Show me an authentic Picasso and I'll show you an authentic fake.

Your criticism of me is like art, your mouth is the canvas, and my fist is the paint.

The artist is free to make a mistake and then sell it.

Art is like a witness, two people look at the same thing and both see something different.

Art is not what you see, but what you think you see.

If your favorite art is the portraits on money then welcome to the art world.

Liberal art is paint under duress on canvas.

Madness it's good for the arts.

The art of diplomacy is part deception just like art is part deception.

Art, it's what you make of it.

Oh what is art?
Oh anything can be art,
Oh art is snow on a snowy day,
Oh why does everyone see it differently?
But to me art is money.

If I knew how to paint I would be broke said to artist.

It is not bad art when the price goes up.

All original art is a copy.

All art is the opinion that is never wrong and never right.

Art makes the simple complicated.

The blind man can't see, and the artist sees what the rest of us can't.

Creativity is art with a high price tag.

DEATH********************************
(Written by Joseph Bonkowski)

Dead men sin no more.

Death is the great forgiver.

The end or your life is just the start of heaven or hell.

If thoughts could kill would there be anyone alive?

The grave will stop a man from stealing, and lying, but not from accounting to God.

It was the best of times; it was the worst of times, depending on death, if you go up or down?

Death; I like to procrastinate on it.

Home sweet home, and soon the graveyard will be home.

Death is what makes life worth living.

You can be on your deathbed and imagine you are on a beach; you can also be on a beach and imagine you are on your deathbed.

Death is not a laughing matter, so laugh while you are alive.

Death makes everybody's I.Q. the same.

If a pastor tells a lie at your funeral it won't get you to heaven.

If you never say die, you still will one day.

Death is the only race I don't mind losing.

A life without any problems shall be in the graveyard.

I'm just trying to outlive the grim reaper.

I hope you learn how to live before you die.

A word to the man that has committed suicide, well I can't tell you, because you are dead.

Death heals all wounds.

Death and taxes are like hemorrhoids and hernias, who needs them?

The person afraid of death is not living.

It's always too late to die.

Live a good life and your obituary will take care of itself.

My money can buy material things, but once I'm dead the only material thing my money can buy is a coffin.

Death is like a game of tag, the grim reaper is "it", and the reaper is chasing you.

You're always at your best when you're the deceased at your eulogy.

I am only defeated when I say I am, and death will be my only defeat.

Dear Grim Reaper,
I have no time for death; make an appointment for forty years from now, call first to see if I'm home.
Thank you,
Still alive.

If the grim reaper lives long enough will he die?

To the liar who lies about lying, one day you will lie in your grave.

God he's not just for the deathbed.

Death forgives debt.

Death, that's life.

A coward dies a thousand deaths, woo-wee I get to die a thousand times!!

Death just stick around.

100 dead people keep a secret better than one live person.

Death is it the last thing you'll ever do?

Make amends before they say A MEN.

You only die once, you only live once.

One thing I recommend in life is that everyone lives before they die.

My tomorrow will come the day I die.

If a man on his death bed had never lived then how could he have died? By not living life while alive.

When I'm dead I won't care what you say about me, until then watch your mouth.

The last will and testament; I have no money and thank you paying for my funeral.

Think well of death, we all have to do it, just once, I think?

Enjoy what you have, it can be gone tomorrow or worse you could be gone today.

I don't mind going to prison, start my sentence anytime after I'm dead.

Death makes all illnesses equal.

If there's never a good time to pray, then you better hope there is a good time to die.

Why doesn't congress pass an anti-death law, making it illegal to die, I always obey the law.

The secret to long life is never to cash in your life insurance.

Everyone thinks today they have a tomorrow.

Suicide is the mistake that can't be erased.

When I'm gone don't ask my friends what I was like, but try to find an enemy of mine.

Until death do us part, and later we will depart.

If you work yourself to death then you will rest forever.

Life sucks, death sucks worse.

If you don't think that anyone will remember you for your loving acts or acts of kindness, then you will just have to include some acts on your tombstone.

The secret to life is to prepare for the afterlife.

When you are on your death bed I bet you won't say "I wish I worked more overtime".

There is truth in the death bed.

Death to me is nothing but a caterpillar turning into a butterfly.

When the sun rises tomorrow you may not rise.

On my tomb stone it shall read "Mind your own business and find another tombstone to read."

Suicide some people are dying to try it.

Death is your farewell performance.

The man that couldn't stop working soon will rests in his grave.

To die young, how many tragedies were missed?

At the end everyone accumulates a head stone.

Do the dead have a long night?

To me, the day, I die is the day the world ends.

I die one day at a time.

I accept the fact that I must die, but just not today.

Birth, stuff happens, death.

Don't die with a lie.

There is no problem that death can't cure except death.

Death is a good excuse not to show up for work.

You die one time, big deal.

The remedy for death is God.

If you think you will find God on your death bed you may die in your sleep?

Death to the person who wants to commit suicide.

Birth and death makes us equal.

We all die alone.

Obituaries are the gossip columns for the dead.

Eat, drink and be merry, for we all have to die.

I bought life insurance, it had a suicide clause in it, and I thought I'm not planning on dying.

Men grow out of watching football when they die.

Honey I'd die for you, but then I would miss you.

Death you could be just one tax payment from it?

Is there life after theft?

Everyone moves when they die.

Are you late to the wake, or do you just wait to become late?

What I am willing to die for is nothing.

A fossil is nothing but a grave marker.

Suicide is a compounded mistake.

Everyone is born, a billion ways to go from here and only one place to go, the graveyard.

Belittle me when I'm dead, not alive.

The dead don't visit me and I don't visit them.

Death turns all smokers into nonsmokers.

Death what good is it? Life insurance.

This life is important, but not as important as the next life.

The lord knows you don't want to work your whole life, so he made death.

Time heals all wounds and so does death.

Born=beginning, life=middle, death=end.

You will be dead longer then you are alive.

Why must a man die? Because he lived.

A true Christian never dies.

Cautious is the person afraid to live and afraid to die.

Long life does not mean you have lived life.

Life is like death, it comes and goes.

The rest home is just a dead man walking.

Death is the great doorway to heaven or hell?

What do living people know about death? I do know to live life while alive.

To die or not to die, when is the question?

I don't hate people who are late said the undertaker.

Death to whatever frightens me to death.

The death of a parent is expected, the death of a child is unexpected, and I expect everyone will die.

Sleep well, live well, and die well.

Why should I go to a funeral, the deceased won't go to my funeral.

Suicide then you are taxed.

If you know where you are going after death, that's God (Good) enough.

Is death a new kind of life? This is the question people are dying to answer.

The grim reaper is our company at death.

There are more people dead than alive; we all will be in the majority one day.

EVOLUTION*********SATIRE********
(Written by Joseph Bonkowski)

I put a one dollar bill in my safety deposit box 30 years ago, and it did not turn into a 5 dollar bill, so much for evolution.

The big bang theory AKA in the beginning God created the heaven and earth.

Monkey see, monkey do, see Darwin.

Some say God is just a tale, I say from monkey to man is a tail.

In India they have monkey gods, and in other parts of the world they have the monkey business of evolution.

Did Darwin come from a monkey? Did he once have a tail? And that is the tail (Tale) of Darwin.

By next year my monkey should be smarter than Darwin.

Lie to me, tell me all about evolution.

God spoke everything into existence, and man speaks of evolution.

Addition, subtraction, multiplication, division, geometry, algebra, trigonometry, calculus, advanced calculus, you see evolution does exist.

Darwin's a chimp off the old block.

If you are looking for the missing link you will find your answer on the first page of the Bible.

Something from nothing, see evolution.

Is the next step in evolution creation?

I don't believe in evolution or the big bang theory, but I do believe in fools.

Evolution made a monkey out of Darwin.

Darwin remembered his childhood when he was a little chimp.

My relatives come from dirt and not a dirty monkey.

God created all things including Darwin.

Before I was saved I believed in evolution, I guess I have evolved.

We need a revolution against evolution.

Darwin's nephew was a chimp.

The three monkeys,
Hear no evil,
See no evil,
And Darwin.

The more I study evolution the more I believe in creation, and the more I study creation the more I believe in creation.

It takes two to monkey around said Darwin.

I don't think Darwin will evolve hell into heaven.

Darwin believed in evolution, it may be possible that only the word "word" evolved? (See John 1:1)

All men are created equal, except for Darwin who came from a monkey.

My genealogy started with Adam and ended with me, and there is no monkey in-between.

Horse thieves and Darwin's relatives both hung from trees.

I haven't evolved enough to believe in evolution.

If you believe in evolution, the second you die is the second you will have evolved enough to believe in creation.

1,2,3,4,5,6,7,8,9, see evolution does work.

If you think evolution made the rocks, then you have rocks (Evolution) in your head.

If you can't find your bible, you won't find the missing link either.

There is no missing link from Adam to me.

Darwin tried to put a monkey wrench in creation, and just wound up being a monkey's uncle.

Darwin would be happy to know the first astronaut was his relative.

If a rock doesn't move in a thousand years, what makes you think it will move in a million years? (Evolution)

Darwin's brain evolved from his ass (Donkey).

Liar, liar, Darwin's paints are on fire along with the rest of him.

What kind of monkey business is evolution?

Darwin did not come up with the theory of evolution by himself, his bother Bonzo helped.

If you believe in evolution then you should know that God has created a fool.

Evolution VS Creation- if creation wasn't first, then evolution could not be.

Darwin told a tale about his tail.

Darwin told a tale about his tail and that's the tale of Darwin.

FAILURE********************************
(Written by Joseph Bonkowski)

If you fail, maybe it's because you fail to try?

I'd rather try and fail than fail to try.

It's not that I don't try; it's that I don't try hard enough.

Why am I the only one on earth with obstacles in my way?

I need someone to blame my failures on, so I blame the government for my lack of ambition.

Don't kick a man too hard when he's down, one day that man may be you.

Mistakes are the product of a lack of logic, reason, common sense and knowledge, and if I'm wrong, that's just one more mistake.

You are the boss of your mind, and you can fire fear and procrastination.

Things may turn out better if you except that things will turn out better.

Success is what you have left after so many failures.

Replace the word can't with can and you can fail all over again.

If you can get up when you're down, you don't notice that everyone around you was down, for its only when you are down you notice others are up.

More mistakes happen to the successful than to the man who has failed.

Winner's peak by doing their best at the right time, and the losers doesn't know what time it is.

Laziness is a short road that never ends.

You will fail every time you don't try.

The world is the great scapegoat for failing.

You hold yourself back better than anyone else can.

Being wrong is not a crime, but convincing yourself that you are then right is criminal.

Recipe for failure, don't give a damn.

Take the stress of success over the fear of failure.

But, and if, are the scapegoats of failure.

When life gives you lemons make lemonade, and life consists of making a lot of lemon aid.

The failure is often someone who has tried the more difficult things in life and has the average results.

A man must be willing to admit his faults, even if it's though no fault of his own.

Success is what's left after many failures.

Fail once shame on you, fail twice shame on me.

Most people don't know how hard it is to be a success, says the successful failure.

Great people adapt, and losers adapt to failing.

Gloom and doom follow the person that thinks it.

Life is not fair, just assume that the next man had a better hand dealt than you did, and deal with it from there.

The lessons in life are less the less you try.

In my mind I never fail, imagine that.

One advantage of being disadvantaged is you have such a little way to fall.

I can do two things at the same time, I can be a loser and not care.

If you use Murphy's Law it will happen.

If it's too easy get ready to fail.

Those who are successful have failed more times than you.

Failure is the foundation for success and I have a large foundation.

Don't think that you are not good enough; others will think that for you.

The only excuse for failure is "I'm dead".

Failure is to excel at doing nothing.

Why do I lose so many win win situations?

Failure yesterday, failure today, failure tomorrow, at least I'm a success at being a pessimist.

Failure = wishes + lack.

Your mother can see the greatness in you, why can't you?

Fail, fail, fail, fail, almost success, fail, fail, fail, fail, success.

I am a winner A.K.A. B.S.

The world has happened to my dreams.

You win a few you lose a bunch.

For every winner there is a loser, I wonder who my winner is.

40 years to climb to the top, and one day to fall to the bottom.

Defeat VS Despair and I don't care.

Tomorrow I will be a winner.

Make a plan, eliminate all of the possibilities for failure, what's left are failures you didn't plan on.

FEAR********************************
(Written by Joseph Bonkowski)

Fear is the name of my prison.

Fear is what we perceive as fear.

Fear is unemployment or working overtime.

I have nothing to worry about, and that's what worries me.

Fear is 99% exaggeration.

I am not afraid to be afraid.

The liar knows no fear.

Fear destroys the one that accepts it.

Fear is one part nonfiction and 10 parts fiction.

Fear is a boomerang that we must all live with.

Tranquility will move over for worry.

Courage is having the courage to push fear aside.

Tranquility doesn't fear fear, you do.

Hell on earth is to fear hell on earth.

Fear of change is the type of fear that stops most of us from changing.

Fear has a place when a lion shows up.

You know to stand up to a bully is the right thing to do, and your fear is your bully.

Fear is a most fearful thing.

I'm 5 feet 10 inches tall, and I worry if fear will get me, I won't stop worrying until I'm 6 feet 4 inches underground.

Fantasy creates both fear and joy.

What is a bully but two fists and one loud mouth?

Fear is what you don't know, knowledge is what you know, then why do so many people fear knowledge?

Fear can imprison you more than a prison can.

Face your fears, face your problems, and face the man in the mirror.

Don't run so fast from fear that you run into danger.

I have a fear of having phobias.

When fear graduates it becomes both fear and worry.

The one hundred dollar traffic ticket is two hundred dollars worth of worry.

Worry is fiction.

Fear lies in the dark and knowledge is a light.

If you are in a hurry you may have some worries.

Fear- What goes up must come down.

I release my worries, and I worry if I did that right?

The strong man can't lift his worries.

I fear that I have no fear.

I fear I will have nothing to worry about if I could just stop worrying.

Fear and worry are shackled together, and the key is only in your mind.

Too worry, what a waste of fear.

Worry won't add one day to your life, but it might take many away?

Oh bee that has no fear,
Oh flea that has no fear,
Oh germ that has no fear,
Oh they are all so small,
Oh maybe my fear is small not tall?

Fear is fiction.

Fear is a rope that can bind you.

Worry is in the storage area in your mind where fear is kept.

Fear, its bark is bigger than its bite.

The coward is always brave in his mind.

The only thing fear is afraid of is you changing your thoughts.

Fear is like a shadow, it can be smaller than the object, or larger than the object, but the actual shadow can't hurt you.

Small things are big troubles in our heads.

I fear that we all have different fears.

Fear is when imagination gets exaggerated.

From heartless to compassion is the bully with a bloody nose.

Fear is the monster in our brain.

Fear stops opportunity.

I'm afraid to think of what might have been if I weren't so afraid.

Fear doesn't stop me, procrastination does.

Fear, most of the time it's all thought.

Fear is the obstacle that stops success.

Imagination creates fear where there is none.

If you don't master fear, it will master you.

If you are afraid to live life, you are already dead.

Afraid, worry, fear, they are all in your head, so keep them out of your bed.

Laugh at depression and depression will join in.

The worry of work is worse than the work.

Fear not the past, present or future, fear only God.

FOOL********************************
(Written by Joseph Bonkowski)

A fool doesn't lack judgment, he lacks good judgment.

I'm too intelligent to be stupid, and too stupid to know it.

There's a sucker born every minute, and a fool born every second.

When the fool and the wise man talk, the fool is the one talking.

The court jester acts like a fool, but it's only an act, and the fool acts like the court jester.

It take's a fool to raise a fool, like father like son.

A fool and his money soon play poker.

Some of us are fools, and some of us are drunken fools.

The fool has no indecision for long.

The fool calls everyone around him a fool and everyone around the fool calls the fool a fool.

You can always tell a fool, but you can't tell him much.

Quit playing while you are ahead and enjoy wisdom, keep on playing and enjoy playing the fool.

The wise man will say I don't know, and the unknowing fool will answer.

For every wise man there is a fool, and for every fool there are two wise men, because the fool counts himself as wise.

The tragedy is not that the fool talks, but that we listen.

I keep telling you, if you have a problem tell it to the fool.

Only a fool risks his life for gold, or fool's gold.

Birds of a feather flock together, the wise are like parrots they often repeat what they hear, the fools are like parrots they often repeat what they hear.

The fool that emulates the wise man deceives himself.

Put a fool in king's clothing and he's still a fool, put a king in fools clothing and he's still a king.

I think there are many people so smart they are dumb.

Fools follies fight.

There's no fool like an old fool, and no friend like an old friend.

If you take advice from a half wit, you may not be far from a half wit.

To all the fools; loan me some money.

Two ½ wits don't make a whole wit.

If you think God is a fool then you are a fool who has fooled himself.

I'm too smart to be dumb, and too dumb to know it.

I have much wit until I do an act of stupidity, and then I'm a half wit.

An educated fool never questions the teacher.

There are no limits to stupidity.

Listen to the fool, answer the fool's questions, and judge not the fool, wish the fool a long life, and then step back from the mirror.

The fool wonders, and the wise man wonders why.

A hardheaded man can wear a hat but not a halo.

The liar lies to who he thinks is a fool, and often that's everyone including himself.

To the person that thinks the world is full of fools, look in the mirror.

Any fool can play four aces; it's what you do with the bad hands that count.

I try to understand the ignorant, and the ignorant try not to understand.

Treat children like children and adults that act like children as fools.

Only laryngitis makes the fool sound wise.

The fool says I can do that, and the wise man says you go first.

It's a rare thing for a fool to admit he made a mistake, and fools are not rare.

God looks after fools, and we are all fools.

A fool and his money, will often loan you ten dollars.

The fool thinks he has wisdom and will never find what he is not looking for.

Fools love to call other people fools, and I can see you're a fool.

Who is the fool? The man that doesn't know or the man who thinks he knows?

The fool takes stupidity to a new level.

To call a fool wise is like calling a dictionary fine literature.

There are plenty of educated fools.

Almost everyone is a smart fool.

The fool thinks everyone is a fool; the fool often has no favorite author, for he has no reason to read a book written by a fool.

The fool makes few mistakes, just ask him.

I was the fool who's money was parted.

I don't think much of the fool, and the fool doesn't think much.

Any fool can be an idiot.

Ignorance is bliss, and the fool has plenty of bliss.

Having a hardhead or having rocks in the head are two different things, I just don't know the difference.

A fool and his money are soon parted, and if you have no money maybe you are the fool?

A fool and his money will soon just be a fool.

The man that speaks when angry only speaks as a fool.

He's only a fool when he's awake.

Anyone that knows it all has a lot to learn.

Wisdom is the choice that every fool thinks he makes.

For the fool to be a wise man, he must first wise up.

The longer you argue with a fool the more of a fool you become.

The wise man that needs no one is a fool.

The fool knows everything except that he is a fool.

I pity the witty fool.

If you want to see someone not as smart as they think they are look in the mirror.

Stay away from the fool, he might be contagious and he doesn't even know it, so I'll try to hang out with the wise, but do the wise think I'm contagious?

The wise man wonders where the fool blunders.

Slander is nothing but a fool talking too fast.

A fool and his idea are soon parted.

The fool thinks he practices wisdom when he speaks, the problem is he speaks.

The fool does not seek advice from his elders and one day he will be an old fool.

The fool tries to balance between heaven and hell, the wise try only for heaven.

Wisdom is the common sense to change your mind; foolishness is the lack of common sense.

Fools rush in and wise men study them.

A fool fools himself.

Work is for fools, then again aren't we all fools?

When a fool speaks it's like Russian roulette, you don't know when he will shoot his mouth off.

Try not to be typecast as a fool.

A fool with a smart mouth thinks he's talking to a fool with dumb ears.

The fool and wise both use four letter words, yet the fool uses more four letter words than the wise.

To get into the middle of an argument makes three fools.

If you know too much to study, then just study what a fool is.

Ain't no fool ever got old.

Fool me once shame on you, fool me twice and I guess I am a fool?

Ignorance is the wise sounding loud mouth.

A fool and his mouth never part.

The fool is in denial are you a fool?

Sometimes it's hard to tell the literate from the illiterate.

To never be wrong is a genius or a fool, but most of the time it's a fool thinking he's a genius.

Loan a fool money and you become the new fool.

I like to think about things twice so I don't become a halfwit.

Comedy; what's so hard about it, just watch a fool.

One fool outside the school leads to two fools outside the school.

The louder the argument the louder the fools.

Always show mercy to the fool, because one day you may be the fool.

I tell you the world is full of fools and only fools call each other fools.

Two fools are better than three.

The right tool for the right job, get a fool to speak out against a dictator.

The fool never says he's a fool, and I'm no fool.

I see a fool claiming to be wise every time I look in the mirror.

The fool leaps first and then looks, his funeral is tomorrow.

The loud mouth boasts about anything except him being the fool.

The clown is a paid fool, do they pay you?

I forgot I was a fool, so now I also have a memory problem.

A fool thinks quickly and a wise man studies quickly.

The fool speaks when he has nothing to say.

Be smart enough to trust in yourself, or foolish enough to trust in others.

Being a fool is so easy the fool doesn't even try to become one.

Only the fool was fooled.

To all the fools who cut school, a simple phrase you must learn, would you like fries with that?

The fool makes the mistake of being right all the time.

A fool and his money did not tithe.

The fool thinks he's wise and the wise thinks he's not a fool.

There's a big difference between playing a fool and being one.

Any fool can be smart at least once.

A fool and his mother are soon parted. (Two meanings)

The fool has the right to speak and I have the right to laugh.

FREDOM**************************
(Written by Joseph Bonkowski)

Preserve freedom at all costs, or it will cost you your freedom.

Freedom without freedom of religion is not freedom.

It's best to wait until the 4th of July to shoot your mouth off.

This country has gone to hell, even the colder parts.

A tyrant is just a bully with an army.

An enforced constitution is worth more than a million deaths, and an unenforced constitution is not worth one death.

I will not take any bribes, this makes me eligible for public office, and it also makes me unelectable.

The freedom to be evil is the freedom to be jailed.

Democracy was assassinated by big business.

Our liberal apathy killed freedom, liberty and justice for all.

I had a dream that all men are equal, that no one has rights.

Only congress, the senate and the president are above the law.

You have rights; you have the right not to question government.

Freedom struggles, losing freedom is no struggle.

If my neighbor's rights interfere with my rights, I don't have the right to kill him, I have the right to tell him, and if he still keeps interfering with my rights, I then have the right to go to jail.

It's easy not to miss what you don't have.

To overlook my rights is to get an overhand right.

I was free to do anything and I did nothing, now I am free to do nothing.

An unenforced constitution is like quicksand, you lose your rights slowly no matter how much you struggle.

Freedom involves responsibility, so be a responsible voter.

Popular vote is popular with me.

I don't count the votes; I vote.

Today the judge is the law, even if the judge has to create his own law.

The right tool for the right job and it's my right to have the bill of rights.

The only way freedom works is when we are all free together.

Freedom gives me the right to tell you my opinion, and the right to walk away when you tell me yours.

Often the nonvoter speaks the loudest, and it's my vote that allows him to do this.

To utter words is your right, please try to utter them right.

To smoke is your right, to not smell it is mine, do you mind.

Revolution is a form of criticism.

True freedom is both free to speak and to act.

It's not just the devil that is trying to violate the bill of rights!

It takes an idiot to raise a liberal, and a liberal to be an idiot.

My logic suffers when I try to think how liberals think.

I want to be free enough to lose my freedoms by my choice, and not by my neighbor's choice.

Nothing stops nothing, and actions stops tyrants.

The scales of justice are not blind; they can see who has the money.

If we ever get a one party system it won't be much of a party for us.

Freedom of speech is not silent.

Quiet is the man that did not vote, and loud is his mouth later.

Freedom means I'm free to make money.

To share and share alike, my rights are your rights.

Freedom; As long as you have it you don't need it.

A tyrant is a bully over the nation.

Reverse treason is what my country has done to me.

Soon the only justice left will be injustice!

If everyone prepares for a revolution today, we will not have one tomorrow.

To lose freedom for a few dollars makes the dollars worth-less.

Voting for the wrong candidate makes you an average voter.

Freedom of speech, we have it, and you used it, so now shut up big mouth.

Good men fight for our rights, giving the lazy man the right not to fight.

When patriots do nothing it is a short time before your rights are worth nothing.

Many men have died for our freedoms, and their names did not make it in the history books, but thanks to them we have history books.

Freedom is what you can do and what you can't do.

To keep freedom, keep your feet on the ground, keep a cool head, and keep one hand on your gun.

The victim in court is the one with the least money.

Money buys an innocent verdict.

I don't care if it kills you to fight for my rights.

Many cowards can kill freedom, only a few brave men can bring it back.

The more patriots the more right, less patriots no rights.

Our freedoms look to me like they are slowly dying one day at a time, I yell this out, but some stupid people using the rights of the 5th amendment told me to shut up.

Not many people know the name of the successful tyrant, but they know the name of the puppet in charge.

History is the opinion of the one with the pen.

A tyrant has one army, and I have one pen.

Only humble to a tyrant when you have a knife for his back.

The brave have died for the freedom of a coward to live.

To establish justice, you must establish a just judge, but who judges the judge?

FREEDOM = WAR

If the freedom of speech is taken from us, the freedom to think is right behind it.

Democracy made possible by the voter, the voter made possible by democracy.

When 2% of the country owns 80% of the country something's wrong, the other 98% must work harder.

The truth shall set you freedom.

Freedom, I lost it at the polls.

I have all the freedoms I want or need until I show up in court.

Many countries vote their freedoms away.

The blind can't see the bill of rights, the mute can't speak the bill of rights, and yet they are included.

When one man owns all the toys, revolution!

Let the world know, the U.S. is a free country, and wants every country to be free, and if your country is not free, we will invade it at gun point to give you freedom.

Not to be free in the east, soon may mean not to be free in the west.

If I am the only man standing up for justice, then I stand alone, and if you don't stand with me it is because you are on your knees!

Conservatively the constitution was written, and liberals limit it.

Let the nation stand anew, vote in a new crooks.

Freedom echoes.

It's too late for peace once you have surrendered.

I would give all my money for freedom, and others would give all their freedom for money.

Woman's suffrage, I vote they shouldn't suffer.

If you don't care about your freedoms, then I must care for you, I won't get a thank you, I'll probably be called a nut, but it is my right to be that nut.

The old laws were made for criminals and the new laws for patriots.

Laws were made to be broken, but by whom?

A dictator will promise you everything and take everything.

My time is valuable, my freedom is valuable, and I'll take some of my valuable time to vote for my freedoms.

It takes courage to stand up for all of your beliefs and a coward to stand up to just some of what he believes.

Every time we change the constitution we must eat some words.

Freedom gives the rights to shape the government, and instead the government shapes us.

One well meaning conservative should be able to outrun four well meaning liberals.

I don't need your permission to obey the 5th amendment, and I don't need your permission not to.

The right of the 5th amendment doesn't make you right? Am I right?

Tyranny brings tears to my eyes.

The stage is set, the fat lady is on stage, the fat lady is about to sing, wait, the fat lady just lost here freedom of speech.

The police are around criminals, I don't like criminals, so I stay out of the donut shops.

The cost to be free is not free.

Silence only gets you in trouble when it's time to speak.

Silence turned the democracy into a dictatorship.

Only in my dreams can I truly be free, and I am free to go back to bed.

Knowing that I have freedom of speech, I say nothing.

What's wrong for one is wrong for all.

Stand up don't shut up.

Money over freedom devalues money.

Democracy gives me the right to vote one crook out and another crook in.

Saying the flag is just a piece of cloth is like saying money is just a piece of paper.

Freedom is not free.

Money can't buy freedom, but it helps to win elections.

Combat terrorism vote for the independent party.

To sell out your own country, you only sell yourself out.

Freedom enslaves me.

Freedom gives me the freedom to be free, boredom gives me the ability not to care, don't confuse the two.

The more freedom rings, the better the tone.

The price of freedom may cost you your life, and without freedom you have nothing to live for.

If you become a quiet lamb, you become good eating.

THE BEST THINGS IN LIFE ARE FREEdom.

He who lives by freedom shall die free.

A weak society has a strong dictator.

Freedom is like a drug, some people can't get enough and others don't even think about it.

I talked all day about my freedom of speech.

America- where's my kickback?

What the court system does illegally is the new legal.

America is freedom for all to pay taxes.

Freedom can only set you free if you have the freedom to enforce it.

The king speaks and it's done, I speak and I'm told to shut up, is this freedom of speech? The king says it is.

They say it is better to work within the system, but that would make me guilty by association.

All laws are written on a teeter-totter and sway with the money.

You are what you speak.

There ain't no pleading the 5th on judgment day.

To aid a criminal makes you an accomplice, and it's illegal, but lawyers do this, is it legal?

To the man that leaves his freedoms with the government, you have none.

Most people don't want to work for freedom, they want someone else to do the protesting, the marches and go to jail, they have the freedom to do this.

Do not judge one another, but yet we vote?

Democracy is the 8th wonder of the world.

Radical thinking doesn't change the world, radical actions do.

The 5th amendment can be loud noise or silence.

A liberal is in favor of free speech as long as it's censored.

Freedom is old, and the illusion of freedom is older.

Freedom is not only the right of free speech, but also the right of silence.

Freedom is one thing, and it's another thing to practice it.

Fear not the constitution, but the ones who enforce it.

Law and order is needed in order to keep the law and order.

I'd fight the few now for my rights, then the millions later.

It is only after a democracy dies that the people notice it.

It's later then the nation thinks.

The pen is mightier than the sword, and the dictator has many pens.

The words of the press are in black and white, my mind is in color.

Freedom is equal in the graveyard.

My full freedom or my full fist.

The crime today, the time tomorrow.

I have but one life to give for my country, so I better get more life insurance.

Man made prisons, man made taxes, man made guns, and a woman made the man.

You don't help freedom grow by putting your head in the sand.

The truth shall set you free, if not try money.

Vengeance is the opinion of the few about justice.

The constitution must come with an army.

An open and shut case depends on if your wallet is open or shut.

Many wars that have nothing to do with freedom are started in the name of freedom.

We have inherited freedom from our forefathers, let's not squander our inheritance.

Democracy falls from within.

A silent majority makes the minority mighty.

The press should be free, and not free to not report.

Don't criticize the freedom of speech or you may not be able to criticize anything.

The tyrant says I'm not under duress.

One man speaks best with a million voices behind him.

The fool voted for the wrong candidate two years ago, and now I know I was the fool.

Tyrants burn bibles, and later they will burn for it.

Take away our Bibles and so goes our liberties.

In anything a bad decision is brilliant with the right press.

Nothing is free, including free speech.

Money tips the scale of justice.

You can't stop the press, for if you try I'll print that.

Do or die time, stand up for liberty or die the slow death of a coward.

The police are corrupt and the U.S.A. is the policeman of the world.

When fighting for your rights, one mouth and two fists go further than two fists.

Nothing is as free as freedom itself.

Speak out now, you may not be able to later, it is later then you think.

My freedom is not up for negotiation, yours may be, but that's only because you allow it.

My views are right, but for freedom to be true, I must give you the right of your views, and then laugh.

Tyrants kiss their donkey, or kick their donkey.

Not all prisons hold criminals, some hold patriots.

If you freely bow down to a dictator you have freely given up your freedoms.

The monster of our freedom is the uninformed nonvoter.

I want to keep your freedom safe, so give it to me and I will put it in a safe.

Unenforced the constitution is just a sheet of paper.

If you stand up for your rights, your rights will stand up for you.

Magic is the ability that the government has to make you think that you are in control.

Justice is not blind; she can see who has the money.

Dictators; They always want something.

When the majority is silent the minority may rule.

The most successful form of a tyrant is the tyrant that puts into your head that he is not a tyrant.

Your children's freedom's depends on your freedoms today.

I have the freedom to enslave my mind.

With great freedom comes great responsibilities, I lost my responsibility with my divorce, except for the alimony.

Does freedom of speech give you the right to tell me what I don't want to hear? I hear it does.

If I could get drunk off of liberty, I would be an alcoholic.

Freedom gives me the freedom not to fight, so you must fight for me, that's my right.

When I stand up for my rights I also stand up for your rights, and if they put everyone in jail that stands up for everyone's rights, the only people left will be on their knees.

Why do so many people want to take our freedoms away? I don't understand it, because some day they may need them?

Freedom costs, not having freedom costs more.

FRIENDS************************************
(Written by Joseph Bonkowski)

A friend is only as good a friend as you are to them.

If a friend finds you, it is often better than you finding them.

All of my friends are honest or really good liars.

It takes two to make one friend.

Treat your friends right and you may have no enemies.

A friend in need shall need nothing.

No friend stands alone.

My mother is my oldest friend.

A fair weather friend will be with you in a rain storm, but only if you have an umbrella.

Eggs are good, bacon and eggs are better, steak and eggs are better yet, and steak with a friend is the best.

I enjoy my friends while they are here, because later I may be the one not here.

Friends find fewer faults in you than you do.

If you can't afford to loan a friend something, you can't afford that friend.

It is illogical why we can pick someone who is less than we are for a friend, even though my friend may think the same.

Friends make the best lovers, and they also make for the best divorce.

The death of a friend need not kill the friendship.

If you like yourself you will always have a friend.

We trust a non-experienced friend over a stranger who has experience.

A friend can break your heart; a friend can mend your heart.

Be content with your friends, and content with your enemies.

An old friend is like a dog, loyal and has your best interests in mind.

Your mind is like a SHIP,
It may become adrift,
You don't want to go down with the SHIP,
And that is why we need friendSHIP.

Help your friends to be better than you and one day they may pull you up.

If a friend takes a side, a friendship may die.

I see said the blind man, only because a friend told him so, and the man with sight did not see, and could not see how good a friend can be.

A friend in need is a friend indeed, but if he is your friend than he should never be in need.

I and a friend walk together, one with head held high, the others head held low, I won't say which is which, but I find more money than my friend.

Don't judge your friends, because the penalty may be living the rest of your life without them.

I count myself lucky when I count my friends.

Both you and your friend will one day die and possibly go to heaven, and I want the best for my friend so he can go first.

I want the best for my friend, so that's why I made him my friend.

An old friend is like glue, they just stick to you.

If a friend tells you "You can't do that", and makes you believe it, then I believe you should get a new friend.

We may not do great things, but we may have great friends.

Honesty makes few friends, but good friends.

The strongest man in the world has the most friends.

Forgive money matters with a friend, because money shouldn't matter.

Appreciate your friends or they may depreciate.

Friends are not perfect, sometimes they have funny ways, always laugh with them and not at them.

Wisdom is knowing that you have a friend before you lose him.

My friends lift me higher, and I lift my friends higher, together we can fly.

Don't love a friend because you need them, need them because you love them.

The road to making a good friend ends with a good friendship.

My friends have no faults, only imperfections.

You can't be everybody's friend, but everybody can be your friend.

We are with our friends more than our family, and this may be because we can pick our friends and not our family.

The person with no friends is not alone, he is very alone.

The best place to take a friend is heaven.

If you lose a friend because you have no money, you have only lost your money.

When you are down a friend will pick you up, and when your friend is down you will pick him up, it should average that you are side by side.

Make a good friend of yourself and you will make many more friends.

I keep only my good friends, they share all my opinions.

Envy breaks up more friendships than men who sink ships.

To err is human, to forgive is a friend.

What has four legs and walks? Your friend.

A friend will pick you up when you are down, even if it pulls him down.

If your friend is not a success, maybe that's because you never tried to make him one?

One friend = 1,000 acquaintances.

If you make God your best friend you can't go wrong.

My broke friends are fair weather friends, and it seems like it's always raining.

One evil friend sinks the friendship.

There's an old Japanese saying "May my enemies get everything they wish", and I wish this for my friends!

Friend or foe, that depends on how many years you've been married?

If everyone you ask says no, you have no friends.

Behind every great man there's a friend.

GAMLBING**********************
(Written by Joseph Bonkowski)

My money belongs in my pocket and not in some gambling casino, and I just wish I had learned this lesson 10 minutes ago.

Gambling is a paradise to some and a pair of dice to others.

Lottery played is not always lottery paid.

You have to play to be paid.

I seemed to have mistaken money for the desert when I was in Las Vegas.

Luck is not only having the best hand dealt to you, but having someone to raise.

In Vegas you can't find a good game of Russian roulette.

Gambling- for every winner there is you.

If you play Russian roulette with yourself, when you win you lose.

Lottery is hope for the dope.

Greed is when more is less.

Baseball is only a game, unless you bet money on it.

Too win and whine, WHY?

I don't make my own luck, I just narrow the odds.

Life is like a card game, you don't know the next hand that you'll get dealt, or when the game will end.

The word quit is not in my house, but I lost my house in a card game.

There is strength in numbers, and 747 straight will get $600.00 worth of strength.

Greed + gambling = broke

If you can afford to gamble, you soon won't be able to.

I voted against gambling, because it's 2 to 3 odds against you becoming addicted.

The only sure thing is that nothing is a sure thing.

I don't know why I lose at so many sure things?

Lucky number 7 came 7 times in a row, and still I threw.

GOVERNMENT********************
(Written by Joseph Bonkowski)

I am the government, and the government takes care of me, I wonder how much more self abuse I can take?

If there is no crisis in your country don't worry the government will create one.

Congress is where liars and thieves meet.

The country moves down when it tries to move left and right at the same time.

The more corrupt the state, the bigger the state of corruption we have.

Big government, big questions, small answers.

In the court system, the truth will not win out over a good bribe.

Do you want to hear a joke? Big government.

Big government is one of many government programs that doesn't work.

If man could have a perfect government he would vote against it.

Big government is a raise for the congress and a tax raise for us.

When big business elects a president it is bad business.

Prosperity = Honest government, I wonder why I'm not prosperous?

Good honest government works off a 5% kickback, dishonest government works off a 10% kickback.

The city, state, and federal government are the three tyrants.

I am not ashamed of my country, but I am ashamed of our leaders.

If I am the government then the government pays taxes?

Kickbacks broke our nations back.

My government does me a favor when they raise my taxes, because I am the government and that way I have more money to spend.

Government policy is to tax and spend while saying they are doing more with less.

I rate my government AAA and the AAA batteries are ready to run down.

My government finds a way to tax me and a way to spend it, and even if I get a tax cut, they still find a way to spend it.

Kickback's kills the nation.

My government believes in capital punishment, they take capital from me and that punishes me.

If you steal from the government, you only steal from yourself.

If the government declares war without my vote, then should I be drafted without my vote?

Let us hope that the government does not get too big for the constitution!

Too many crooks spoil the country.

The president sets the presentient.

The government lies, if they told me the truth I would not believe them, so could they just tell me the truth?

The government is a good plan on paper.

I wish they had a government program that made government programs go away.

The smaller the government the larger my wallet is.

The government is corrupt and I won't do anything about it, maybe that's why they're corrupt?

A corrupt government COSTS!!

Big government, it will never work.

If I divorce my government can I get half my taxes back?

Big government the only good it can do is no good.

The freedom of the press is free to print anything it wants that is government approved.

The idiot in charge I voted for, because I didn't want to vote for the other idiot.

You can't fix all the laws by passing new ones.

The government has silenced me, now PLEASE kill the audit.

The government works because, the people have blinders on, and so does the government.

Part of the job of government is to lie, and we are the government.

I am the government and that's why I spend so much.

Beware your enemies may accuse you of doing what they are doing.

If you think government is the answer then you have the wrong answer.

The government is like my wife; it takes my money and tells me what to do.

A country divided will not stand, money divided will stand.

The government is only as strong as the people's government education.

The larger the government's responsibility is the smaller the government's accountability is.

E=MC2 unless the government gets its hands on it first.

Every now and then the government must defend itself against itself.

Big government,
Big business,
Big corruption.

The constitution gives me the right to a bill of rights, the bill of rights gives me the right to stand up for the constitution.

The enemy is coming; the enemy is coming, and its big brother.

No government can print enough money to print its way out of debt.

If congress created the national debt, than let them pay it.

In times of great moral crises, the government makes my mind up for me.

We the people are the government, and what does the government do?
Print money.

Big government is the greatest thing since white bread, and white bread is no good for you.

A one world government would be one big headache.

In the United States there are three parts to the government, corruption, kickbacks, and taxes.

The more I study the way government works, the more I wish I didn't study.

The people make up the government, and I am part of the people, what a bad job I am doing.

The self-destruction of a country starts by just caring about only what happens to you.

When the country is in a hard time, you can always count on the government to make it worse.

Big government, big business, and big kickbacks.

I have a stalker that follows me, and keeps track of me, and I call my stalker the government.

The government is a dangerous form of protection.

It is our incompetent government that prints money backed only by confidence.

The government is the 2nd most dishonest thing man ever made, the 1st is taxes.

I am the government and that's why I am in debt.

GUNSSEE WAR********************
(Written by Joseph Bonkowski)

Many people shoot their mouths off about gun control.

Sometimes to keep your gun you must be willing to use it.

If you try to take away my 5th amendment you will get my six shooter amendment.

A thief won't have to steal my bullets.

The hands make guns and the tongue make war.

It's not the gun that does the crime; it's not the gun that does the time.

Freedom is an illusion without guns.

I should not have to bite the bullet to keep my gun.

The 2nd amendment gives me the right to defend the 2nd amendment.

Peace on one hand and a peacemaker in the other.

Guns stop freedom, guns give freedom.

True and false are opposites unless the man with the gun says differently.

The right tool for the right job, so don't bring that knife to a gun fight.

My gun will be my freedom maker to all the freedom takers.

One slingshot per enemy and I have many enemies, two guns per enemy and I have no enemies.

Home is where my gun is.

Son of a gun if you'll take my gun.

Gun control makes a robber a lion.

If God blessed me with a gun, those trying to take it should be ready to see if god will bless them?

Owning a gun may not get me to heaven, but it can send you to hell.

My gun is my freedom machine.

Cast me off by gun point, and face me later by gun point.

If you take my gun away,
You take my freedom away,
And you must take my life away,
Or I will take your life away,
So please just go away.

Paradox- Guns start wars, guns stop wars.

A gun can make a lamb a lion, or get a lion to cry'en.

They take your gun first and your religion second.

If you think you can take away my gun, then my ideas are the bullets.

My gun is gold, and silver the bullets, and the silver bullet is gun control.

Because I have my peacemaker, I don't need my peacemaker.

A hidden gun speaks loudly later.

One gun or one pen can change the world.

The mouth is like a gun, loaded and ready to shoot.

I have the illusion that I have rights, and my illusion will die when they take my gun away.

My gun will decide right from wrong.

HABITSEE PROCRASTINATION*******
(Written by Joseph Bonkowski)

Maybe you can read this chapter on procrastination later?

I have a habit of not breaking my habits.

Fat people, it's the lack of will power that we can see.

Your diet willpower always starts at the next meal.

When you drop a bad habit, it makes tomorrow today.

Saving is a habit, and so is got to have it.

I saw a nun wearing a large hat, I think it was just a habit she had.

To my alcoholic friend, I'll be your best friend when you decide that alcohol is not your best friend.

To stop smoking is easy; I've done it 7 times.

I push my bad habit everywhere I go in a wheelchair named tomorrow.

An excuse is a crutch for my habit.

I don't know if my waist wears a belt from gluttony or greed?

My habit is procrastination.

If your habit plans your life, plan to get rid of your habit.

Don't let your habit follow you to bed or it will follow you to your grave.

Death is the habit breaker.

After just one day I went to visit my old habit.

The easiest habit to break is one you don't have.

A successful diet doesn't start tomorrow; it starts at your next meal.

Smile one day and it may become a habit.

The guillotine is not the best anti-smoking device, but it works.

It's much harder to break my habit than yours.

If you want a friend to stick with you through thick and thin, get a habit.

To break any habit, you must first break it in your head.

You can break any habit you don't have.

A habit is a form of slavery.

Cigarette smokers drag their butts.

My addiction is my habit, and my habit is my addiction, at least I will always have company.

All habits will be broken tomorrow.

Smoking cigarettes is like playing Russian roulette; you don't know which cigarette will kill you.

Greed is the habit that stops us from breaking our habit.

To cheat while trying to break a bad habit is the habit you first must break.

Money is sometimes an addiction.

A habit is a comfortable friend, a friend that has over-stayed its welcome.

A vice is a bad habit or something wicked or evil, we have a vice president.

Skinny people lose weight, and fat people claim to lose weight.

If your habit is giving into your habit you will always have your habit.

Don't start, won't finish. (Two meanings)

HAPPINESS*************************
(Written by Joseph Bonkowski)

Liquor is happiness in a bottle to some, and the devil in the bottle to others.

No one is as happy as they can be.

Copy the happy with a smile.

Be unhappy tomorrow.

The difference between happiness and unhappiness is un.

Am I happy?
Am I free?
Am I free to be happy?

You can't buy a smile because it costs nothing.

There is no such thing as being overdue to be happy.

Give the gift of a smile and get back the gift of a smile.

Please you and you please the one that counts.

You can't hide happiness.

Happiness is more now than never.

If happiness starts at some point in the future, it will never arrive.

I can think,
I can do,
I can think I can make myself happy,
And I think you can to.

Happiness is what you get when you turn unhappiness upside down.

Enjoy joy.

A bad day starts in your head, and so does a good day.

Most people would rather walk a mile than give a smile.

Both happiness and depression are both in your head and of freewill, am I crazy because I don't know why so many people choose depression?

To be happy what is stopping you is you.

Happiness is the ability to temporarily forget your problems.

Save your sorrows for tomorrow.

The pursuit of happiness starts with a smile.

Adopting a happy attitude is not up to anyone else.

Happiness is something someone can't give you or take from you.

Happiness is so much better when you try it.

Enjoy what you don't have, examples; time not in prison, time not in a wheel chair, constant pain, on a death bed, so enjoy.

A smile on your face may delay sorrow for today and tomorrow.

If you learn how to be happy when you are down, then you may never be down.

Two twins, one poor and happy, and the other rich and sad, which one would you rather be?

A smile when in great distress and it becomes just distress.

Money can't buy happiness, because you never have enough money.

Happiness is so simple it's complicated.

A happy person finds someone to love, and often doesn't know they are happy due to the arguments.

Happiness knows how to play hide and go seek.

Forgive me for not being happy for yesterday for I said I would be happy today.

It sounds too simple to be true, but happiness is what you think it is.

Insane in the brain is said to be the crazy man laughing, but he knows the ones not laughing are insane.

Now is the time to be happy, for our time will soon be up.

Happiness is only complicated in your mind.

Youth is happy up until about the time they start to pay taxes.

If you think happiness is too hard to find then it will be.

Distressed, wear a blindfold for one hour, you'll feel better in minutes.

One small secret to happiness is to laugh with others, and if others don't laugh, laugh by yourself and others will join in.

My job stops me from being happy, and I am happy to have a job.

Joy is the poor person's money.

If you never smile, it's not the worlds fault.

LIE**********************************
(Written by Joseph Bonkowski)

Why lie when you can bend the truth?

I can't tell the truth from non-truth, but I know a lie when I hear one.

Dead men tell no lies, unless they lie about being dead?

Whenever I lie I try to be as truthful as possible.

I think part of the job of government is to lie, and I am part of the government.

The more I lie, the younger I get and the more I own.

Lie, lie, lie, he lies so much I wouldn't believe him if he said he was lying.

Does a lie lie in you?

If I lie I'm human, if you lie you're a liar.

The only fault I have is lying. (Three meanings to this unless I lied?)

Speak the truth about a lie.

I can tell a small lie or a BIG PREVARICATION.

I speak the truth; I just don't do the truth.

My sanity is a lie, but I believe it.

If it's hidden it may be hidden in plain sight?

I don't lie, but I am a member of the liars club, did I just lie to you?

I lie to myself all of the time, but I never lie to others.

Lies travel faster than the truth.

A lie is the doorway to hell.

Always tell the truth about lying.

99% of the truth is still a lie, or is 52%?

Old age you can always lie about. (Two meanings to this)

Lie lie I guess I'm the one that ate the pie.

A liar can lie about being a liar.

When you lie to yourself, almost everyone knows it.

A lie plus a dollar and you'll still have a dollar.

His word is as good as a boomerang.

I only lie to get a job, and I think that's part of the job description?

As long as I know how to lie, I will always have friends in high places.

If you master the language of illusion, then you have found a second way to lie.

Two lies don't make the truth.

I only lied to prove I didn't lie.

Before you lie to someone act like that someone is God.

Someone I once knew lied.

A lie can have a long arm.

A lie can travel faster than a speeding bullet and hurts more than one.

The liar guards his ears because he knows what comes out of his own mouth.

I will never lie again if I just lie about lying.

If a man steals, he will lie, and he may lie about stealing?

I trust my government, and I trust they will always lie.

I can't read or spell, but I can write a lie.

The older I get the more I can lie about my age.

One lie is worth a thousand words.

There will be no liars club meeting this April first??

The know it all lies to himself first, and to others later.

Except a lie as the truth and you only lie to yourself.

The less you promise the less you lie.

There is no such thing as a liar's club, just ask any member.

The truth is not hidden it's just surrounded by lies.

I did not lie, I just misquoted myself.

A leopard can't change his spots, but he can lie about his spots.

We play poker with God when we lie, he can see our hand and still we bluff.

To lie to yourself can make for a good night's sleep.

All words are true, and it is mans arrangements of the words that make them lies.

If you quote a liar, the quote may be wrong.

Liberals claim they do not lie, but they do deceive.

Smoking cures cancer,
Smoking cures cancer,
Smoking cures cancer,
Tell a lie long enough and people believe it.

You can lie your way into hell.

To add to the truth just doesn't add up.

If you believe a lie and tell a lie, is it a lie?

You don't have to lie about the truth.

A lie can't be the truth, even if you lie about it.

The only way a liar is my friend is if he is a very good liar.

Children tell the truth, adults tell some truth.

Everyone is equal, that's a lie, because my lies are not equal to yours.

To the liar the whole world is his mouth.

The pursuit of truth is often covered with lies.

LOVE AND MARRIAGE***************
(Written by Joseph Bonkowski)

Fear is learned and love is earned.

The biggest fights start over the smallest things.

Love can't hide in your heart.

More men are trapped with lipstick than shotguns.

Sex makes a man do things; lack of sex makes him do more.

Absence makes the heart grow fonder, so my wife of forty years, stay away a little longer and let my heart grow really fond.

She was a virgin the last 3 times I had sex with her.

A man can be happy with any woman that he picks, provide that he doesn't know she picked him first.

A man is a man,
And a mouse is a mouse,
Why did my wife throw me out of the house?

Love speaks from the heart, and the head speaks from heartbreak.

You did not marry an old man, you married someone 28 years older than you.

The fool plus one is better than the wise man plus none.

When in love the heart controls the mind and the mind doesn't mind.

To never love is the mistake someone must never make.

I believe in every marriage that at least one of them should be happy.

Without love life is not worth living, without living life is not worth loving.

A leopard can't change his spots so don't marry one.

Love doesn't change, but the weight of love does.

Too willingly alter ones opinion when in love, makes you in love.

Appearances are often deceiving said the bride to the groom.

Love makes us a fool from 12 to 50 years of age, and from 50 on we envy that fool.

Good love is both give and take, better love is give and give.

Marriage is sometimes charity or chastity.

Unfounded love is seldom found.

We were both 21 years old when we got married, now I'm 50 and she's 37.

There are two things wrong with marriage, the husband and the wife.

It takes two to argue and one to apologize.

From sweet wine to sweetheart.

Two love birds must fly together to stay together.

Love means to always leave the seat down.

70 X 7 and still I haven't learned how to put the seat down.

It takes two to love, me and my mirror.

What have I done for love? I have not killed myself and I have not killed her.

I love to hate a love hate relationship.

Love is saying you're sorry even with your foot is in your mouth.

Love is when you fool yourself and can't see that you are acting like a fool.

Love is one addiction that I don't mind being addicted to.

The best way for a woman to be totally in charge is when the man doesn't know it.

Two lonely people make one couple.

The trouble with marriage is you can't listen your way out of one.

What little strength a woman needs to move a mountain, all she need say is honey will you move it.

When in love O.K. is perfect.

Ugly is the woman not willing to make-up. (Two meanings)

The way to a man's heart is just below his stomach.

I used to do everything right, then I got married.

Familiarity makes a marriage, and a baby carriage.

The bachelor knows not what he has missed or does he?

Raising children can be hard; not raising children can be harder. (Two meanings)

The best way to manage your wife is to ask her.

Love is a good four letter word, the bad four letter words are, snow, rain, cold, boss, and work.

Since I don't have a life,
And I don't have a wife,
There's nothing for me to do but be blue.

I would never take my ex-wife to court, she can drive herself.

A 100 pound girl can lead a 200 man around better than a 300 pound man can.

When you add to love you get it back multiplied.

Love, for every attraction there is an equal and opposite attraction.

The man is the home builder, and the woman is the home maker.

Marriage is the most expensive sex that money can't buy.

The only place that you can run from love is to a broken heart.

In marriage an aspirin a day still keeps the sex away.

Women only want your company when you own one.

The smart girl plays dumb.

Logic and reason doesn't limit love.

Love is blind, but lust has eyes.

Tough love is the love that temporary hurts both people.

If marriage isn't like heaven get the hell out.

Women want to change a man, and a man wants to change the channel to football.

A women's work is never done and her job is to nag.

I love my ex-wife; I just didn't like telling her that.

A marriage made in heaven, and a divorce made in hell.

Love is a beautiful thing, but not all beautiful things are loved.

I was dating an old looking 25 year old, and I found out I had dyslexia.

To keep love you must give it away.

Love is when 2nd best becomes the best.

Tough love lasts forever.

A broken heart needs not a by-pass, but not to be passed by.

Love is a present that you find in yourself.

A friend is someone who will bring you down to size when you get too big, and build you up when you get too small.

How many times can a virgin be a virgin? That depends on how well she can act.

I was happy to be in love,
I was happy to be out of love.

True love is to torment each other.

Marriage is give and take, she gives the orders and he takes them.

Which is more important love or wisdom? If you picked love it is the start of wisdom.

Lovers are like cops and robbers, some good and some bad.

A strong man is always stronger with a strong woman.

I am the man in the marriage and I would like to be the one to make the mistakes.

Men or hens? That depends on who rules the roost?

The trouble with a lady dating an older man is sometime the man doesn't own enough.

There is not I or U in Love.

Women rule behind the scene, sometimes they know it, and sometimes they show it.

The harder the heart the harder the head.

Free love is the most expensive.

Guard thy heart well for it leads to the wallet.

Ugly and pretty have the same bad habits and I say pretty doesn't have any bad habits?

I once suffered because I was not married, and now I am married and know what real suffering is.

Marriage is the great catch-22.

When lovers break up,
The truth comes up,
And they still make up.

Love is both friend and foe.

Of course I got a divorce, she reminded me of my feminine side.

People in love and people not in love, and each are feeling sorry for the other.

And old shoe is like an old wife, you get comfortable with it.

I would kill for her,
I loved her until I died,
Not only could her looks kill,
But so could her gun that killed me.

Time alone makes for good times when together.

Marriage is a long time to be on a lease.

Your heart has a mouth when in love.

Without love you are a looser.

In love you must sometimes be apart to be closer.

You hold my hand,
You hold my heart,
You are my sweetheart.

When I work I think of home, when I'm home my wife makes me think work wasn't so bad.

Do we love because we hate the loneliness?

When playing in the card game of life, the king is higher than the queen unless you marry it.

The only thing wrong with a virgin is she lies too much.

The only thing I don't understand about love is love.

Love and anger are both boomerangs.

When two become one its marriage, when one comes two it's a split personally.

Marriage is like my favorite book title, "War and Peace"

IF unhappy is the marriage,
And IF unhappy is the sex,
How happy the divorce is.

It takes work to make a marriage work.

If you want her to love you ignore her,
If she still doesn't love you adore her.

If you want to know what I'm thinking, ask my wife.

If you are married and fight it sounds about right.

The girl has a reputation, she also has a kid.

They have a word for a woman that controls a man, its called reality.

Most women can't make up their minds, but they sure can make up your mind.

My wife suffers from cramps, and I do not, so we both suffer from cramps.

Sex in a marriage is a number between 5 and 7.

Superman lost ½ his powers, he got a divorce.

Unrestrained love may lead to a restraining order.

A successful marriage is getting along while arguing.

You don't have to chase a girl you already have.

My girlfriend said think with your heart, so I broke up with her.

If she's a weeper don't keep her.

Love birds are good,
The peace dove is good,
And a stool pigeon will squeal on a jail bird.

If you are married your standards are too low, if you are single your standards are too high.

I was walking with my girlfriend, when a bee made my honey run.

This is a man's world, I know because my wife said so.

117

She claims she's beautiful, graceful, attractive, affectionate, loving, a delight, and she's also says she's modest.

Your world revolves around the one you love.

I have tamed a dog, I have tamed a lion, and a woman has tamed me.

To love is to trust the key to your heart with someone else.

Beware young man, a woman with brains and beauty may only have beauty?

In marriage two become one, and the one is in charge.

The best way for a poor person to marry rich is for the poor person to first become rich.

Love is when you both decide to do the worrying for each other.

Love takes two, divorce takes one.

Love is what you see when your eyes don't see someone as they are.

Without love you are not alone, you are very alone.

Love and lost, only a few letters difference, only a few love letters difference.

** MISCELLANEOUS*********************
(Written by Joseph Bonkowski)

You can start over any day of your life except for tomorrow.

You don't have to be blind to be blind.

It takes good acting to act like a ham while in a chicken suit.

Things are often so simple it's complicated.

I can take criticism, but can you take a punch?

Optimist, mediocre, pessimism.

I don't mind growing older; I just don't want an old person in the mirror staring back at me.

I think therefore I am. I think?

In hard times don't get hardheaded.

The fame with no name you can't blame. (The real working power is behind the scene)

I invited some fools to my party and no loud mouths, somehow nobody showed up.

The louder you speak doesn't make you more right.

Starting a diet after desert is better than starting a diet tomorrow.

Life is like a boat, and I'm not the only one on the boat, and I blame the captain for why the ship is sinking.

Headaches are all in your head.

I was asked to sing karaoke, I requested Beethoven's 5th symphony.

Pay attention and later your attention will pay you.

The more opportunities you make the more that will come.

I see said Edison.

I don't understand why I don't understand?

I had a car accident, my insurance rates went up, and so I crashed my car again.

I'll tell you a secret, I can't keep a secret.

Stand tall before a bully one time or stand down to him a thousand times.

A big stick talks best to the bully.

I can read you like a book because I read between the lines.

I will try to think of the unthinkable.

If you settle for second place, you probably will not finish in the top 10.

If you regret losing one day of your life, your regret may make you lose every day.

Many letters make a letter.

Anything only satisfies for a while.

I had a daydream about a nightmare.

Today is the only day you can live.

A short stay leaves a good impression.

Actions speak louder than words and words can start actions.

A halo won't fit on a swelled head.

The customer is always a pain in the butt.

The stool pigeon,
Put him on a stool,
Put a rope around his neck,
Kick the stool out from under him,
And see if the pigeon can fly.

My neighbor is in labor, should I help him? For he has helped me, I guess one day I'll start to help my neighbor, but for now I will just let my neighbor labor to put up that tall tall fence.

Haste is a hasty mess.

If you want to improve the world, improve yourself.

Knowing when not to be humble is the beginning of many problems.

The news is the lie that most people believe.

Genius or insanity, it's just a point of view.

The world looks the same to everyone in the dark.

Think of all the stupid things you've done in life, and you say you're the one to judge.

Winning by cheating is still winning; but, cheating yourself.

News- the real news is what the news doesn't tell you.

Tag, your it, and if not the tag will read made in china.

The good old days are now.

Children want to become adults, and adults want to become children.

I think Beethoven's 5th could use the 5th amendment, I know I need a 5th to listen to it?

Revenge let it go, otherwise it's their revenge.

A man with two feet on the ground can't jump far or fall far.

Skill = practice + practice.

Relax, go to the park by choice, or go to the hospital later.

Work hard so you don't have to work hard.

Life often ends just before we plan to start living it.

Life is short and careers are long, so don't make a career out of your career.

Don't make a job out of your work.

Stupidity can be brilliant as expressed by the news.

Smile awhile.

A short argument makes for a short memory.

When evil wins evil loses.

The first fist that fights has the might.

Backaches are headaches.

I waited so long I had patience.

Patience is a virgin.

I dreamt I had insomnia.

Talk, walk, but know when to run.

We all want quiet until we get it.

The risk is what people remember.

To enjoy is a simple thing, it's so simple we think its work, and that's why many of us don't enjoy.

To accept growing older makes it easier, not to accept growing older makes it easier.

Two lent out, one returned.

It takes hard work to work you to death.

My delusion is my illusion.

Two people can think better than one and three people can argue more than two.

Sad clouds bring rain.

Wow! She's beautiful, on a scale from 1 to 10 she's and 11 with 7 being the highest on the scale.

I'm not an idiot, I just do stupid things.

I would like to tell you a secret, but it's a secret.

He has a twin brother that looks just like him.

Experience costs.

Experience costs, inexperience costs more.

Age is the number that you make of it.

I'd like a second chance to make a first impression.

Kind words may cost you if it's a lie, kind words may cost you if not a lie.

A long agreement makes for a short memory.

The weather man says rain this afternoon; it looks like 6:00 A.M. will be this afternoon?

A career you love pays better than a career you hate.

It's not what you do; it's what you make of what you do.

You talk a good show and do nothing for the meeting like the rest of us.

Perception as I see it is me not making mistakes.

If everyone that ever did anything wrong was in prison we would all be in prison, and if everyone judged themselves, no one would be in prison.

Subtitles on movies, if I wanted this I would have read the book.

The nuthouse is full of genius.

And eye for an eye, a tooth for a tooth, see an optometrist and a dentist.

Try to impress yourself and you may impress others.

I see things differently as an adult, I'm taller.

No invention is ahead of its time, it's just that everyone else is behind the times.

Gossip is a condition of the brain that affects the ears and mouth.

Before you walk a mile in another's man's shoes, make sure they are your size.

Get in on the ground floor, that's the only place the entrance is.

If you got the smaller end of the wishbone, then you should have wished for the larger end.

Some buy and some fly.

It's not the economy; it's just that no one has any money.

Stand tall for what you believe, and if you get in trouble over it, I didn't tell you that.

Don't take advice on dieting from a fat man.

Win or lose, the difference is often how much we try or don't try.

When you are traveling forget to pack your bad attitude.

Don't just live, live life.

It's not how you stand; it's what you stand for.

The past has passed away.

A question is only difficult if you have a questionable answer.

Bringing joy to others will rub off on you.

An incorrect answer is the correct answer to a different question.

To be correct is the opinion of the holder of that opinion.

Tough times T.S.

If you can't escape from what is chasing you, then you will discover it is you.

I am turning 50; I'm turning 50 years young.

Fifty and fine opens more doors than forty and fat.

Don't judge a man's word by today, but by today and yesterday.

It's not only what you do, it's what you don't do.

The worse things in life are free.

Often taking your time will give you more time.

If you don't know what's up, shut up.

When one door shuts use the key of knowledge to open another.

I'm not interested in hanging out with you dumb liberals on college campus, I'd rather hang out with my smart conservative friends at the bar.

There's a lot of Latino's, so I took up Latin.

Circumcision is one thing, castration is another.

Gossip is when your ears talk to your mouth.

Whores are worth a dime a dozen, and I don't have a dime.

Tell the loud mouth that less is more and give us more.

What I hate about work is working.

Sleep, if you think about it you can't.

That reminds me of the time I can't remember.

My excuse seems small to you and large to me.

It's not how tall you are, but how you measure up.

If you have insomnia, sleep on it.

I am a benevolent hypocrite.

Acting is just an act, and it helps to act your way through life.

The best actor can fool himself.

Get over it before your head stone gets over you.

I am a typecast actor; I act for the same type of green.

Endurance prevails and it never fails.

To all liberal votes, I hope you don't get what you voted for, but you will probably get more than you voted for.

To the brown nose at work, don't you wish the boss wiped better?

Noise makes the neighbor's fence taller.

I'm at peace with myself, companionship is O.K. but she must leave in the morning so I can have peace with myself.

I love you are three powerful words, and so is I hate you.

To think is to be.

The man that switches his job often will never find the greener grass.

When you look back at your life don't let it stop you from going forward.

The older I get, the better I get, and the better at deceiving myself I get.

A diet starts in your head, then to the lips, and then to the hips.

In life 90% of the blame is on you, and we blame 90% on others.

We all can imagine more bad things that can happen to us than can actually happen to us.

I was appropriately being inappropriate.

He who counts his blessings is rich.

Ask for more than you want, and you may get more than you want.

I heard of Mark Twain, but who is Samuel Clemens?

Please quote me right, unless it sounds better misquoted.

In the good old days everything was older.

Don't let the person with a chip on his shoulder put a straw on your back.

A man is like a grape, he whines (wines) over sour grapes.

Imagination is a beach house, reality is my house.

To the old person, you'll never be younger then now.

From boy to man; man how the toys have changed.

An honest man in doubt is worth more to me than a dishonest man with his mind made up.

If you never change your mind, then look for a mule in the mirror.

Speaking in public is just like talking to a bunch of people.

If you would look at the future as a bright light, you wouldn't think of the past as being so dark.

Patient now and impatient later.

First try to talk to your evil co-worker, if talking doesn't work, then take him to lunch and let him eat a knuckle sandwich.

If it looks like a lion but doesn't sound like one, leave quickly.

Caution youth leads to old age.

A good new year's resolution is to get one year older this year.

Intelligent life fears God, the rest don't think about hell.

I only read books with happy endings, and I only read the last page.

Sticks and stones may break my bones; but, no medical will always hurt you.

One night's good sleep is worth more than two night's bad sleep.

I can't stress the fact that what stresses you may not stress me.

The future comes quickly and leaves quickly.

Your mouth let the skeleton out of the closet.

Old folks don't die young.

If they can't make you angry, it will probably make them angry.

It's not over till it's over sang the fat lady.

Everyone drives faster than the speed limit, sometimes it's a good thing that all laws are not enforced.

When I do the math, I don't understand the math.

Food + greed = fat

If you think drugs are the answer, then you have the wrong question.

Work hard to make life easy.

The longer you talk the more it sounds like a story.

Life's lessons start when you do nothing and the doctor slaps you.

If you hit your enemy with everything that you have, you may find out that he is trying to do the same.

The nonsense you talk is starting to make sense to me.

Try to get along with your neighbor at least well enough for him to help you build a fence.

I am not a philosopher I think.

Poverty is not when you have a chicken in your pot, but when you don't have a pot to chicken into.

If less is more then I have more in my wallet?

I hate people who hate others.

Silence is golden, that's why it costs so much per ounce.

Travel makes you home sick; too much travel and you might get sick of home.

Say something constructive not destructive or else shut up.

If life gives you lemons, then you probably have a sour puss.

Life, it's much better when you live it.

I would like to leave the world better than I found it, but I don't know who to slip the money to?

Anything looks easy to the person who has never done it.

I'm not psychic I'm psycho.

The only thing wrong with a yard sale is more grass to cut.

One of the first steps to being a man is to buy your own shoes.

A picture is worth a thousand words, but please don't show me any pictures of your kids.

If you think the book looks too thick it is.

To think is art from the mind.

If you fight fire with fire you might get burnt.

The wind blows and I don't know where it goes?

Cherish before you perish.

The art of thinking can make complicated problems simple and simple problems complicated.

Greed is first a thought.

Exercise starts tomorrow, or Friday for sure.

Your future is just one second away.

The liberal's point of view has blinders on and the conservative point of view handcuffs.

The liberals claim everyone is equal but insist on giving more rights to some than to others.

Liberals like to prey on those who pray.

The words never spoken are sometimes best.

Silence is the ability to hold your job.

I put up with less when I try to please less.

I try to stay above average, and I try not to grade on the curve.

Silence is just frozen words.

The greed of a company can sometimes close the company, and the greed of the workers can sometimes close the company, greed has plenty of company.

Greed is when more is more.

Do well; your relatives may spend it well when you are gone.

Old age is living one day at a time and many (one) days.

The man that talks a good show doesn't have much to show.

The trouble with a loud mouth is his foots always in his mouth.

The trouble with a loud mouth is your ear is too close to his mouth.

Lazy people don't waste there life by working, they just waste there life's.

Think twice, speak once.

Life is like a stop light, life changes, life goes on, take caution in life, life stops, and then life goes on.

To quote another is to give thanks for their wit.

Dew to the weather rain.

Doing something with nothing is what the boss expects.

The future for everyone is all the same, unknown.

A journey of a thousand miles starts with the first thought.

The reason you can't read anyone's mind is a man's head is too hard and a woman can't make her mind up.

You are not free until your mind is free.

Sometimes we over think a problem and that's why we can't find the answer, I think, or do we under think it, let me think on it??

Too much pleasure may become displeasure.

Learn how to stand on your own two feet or learn how to beg on your own two knees.

Don't call me a male chauvinistic pig, because I think women are smarter than men at anything underhanded.

Enjoy every minute of life for this may be your last minute?

Sometimes an idiot just needs an education.

We all imagine we can, and act like we can't.

Tomorrow will come, even if you don't pay your bills today.

To be good is one thing, to be great is another thing, and to give up is still another.

History repeats, and it can also be changed by re-writing, history does not repeat.

The longer an argument goes on the louder it gets.

The prisoner is truly in prison when he can't dream of being free.

We can see that often ancient history is current history.

Wise words spoken are often not wise words followed.

Heredity is a form of inheritance.

The blind man is king in a power failure.

Action today makes less action for tomorrow.

If the north is too cold and the south is too hot, then try east and west.

Why buy retail when you can buy wholesale, that's how I buy my problems.

Grow up and grow wise.

He was married to his money, and death was his divorce.

Greed has a large appetite.

In my mind I'm a lion, in reality I'm a lamb.

Prejudices & gossip- what else would you talk about on your break?

Hair evolution, missing, black, brown, grey, silver, white, thinning, missing.

Too stay out of trouble stay home.

Don't regret forget.

If the liberal could think, he wouldn't be a liberal.

Man does not live by bread alone, he needs money to buy the bread, so he needs a job, he has to pay taxes, and all he wanted was some bread.

Today is tomorrows yesterday.

A hand out doesn't impress the poor but oppresses the poor.

If you are retired, are you tired for a second time?

The word noun is not a person, place or thing.

Every bag has a hole at the top.

My concern with you is that I am unconcerned for you.

Often we fall at our high point in life because we are not looking to fall.

Time will pass and so will gas.

Justice swings with money.

The faster you go in the wrong direction, the longer it takes to get there.

Things didn't pan out for the chef.

You get what you look for.

A short jest is best.

Tomorrow is the day that will never come, even if you wait 24 hours.

Insanity is needed to be a genius.

It's hard to eat crow with your foot in your mouth.

When making a phone call, the dime is mightier than the dollar.

You can only see light in the darkness.

100 times out of 100 times if you take a 50/50 chance you will average 50%.

If you would shut up we'd have silence.

A hard rock makes a good chair when you're tired.

It takes Father Time to weather a storm from Mother Nature.

When in a bad time, think of a good time.

The flea market, a buyer and a seller, one or two suckers?

I think I might hate indecision.

I'm not complaining I'm criticizing.

I'll fight anybody anytime, but it must be in my mind only.

Work sucks, and unemployment sucks worse.

To my old math teacher, if I have two fists and you have one mouth, what is the ratio of fist to mouth?

No bank can hold one minute of time.

There's strength in numbers, 19 inch biceps should be number enough.

Live your day so you can sleep at night.

You can't get done until you get begun.

Living and life are two different things.

Something accomplished with your hands is better than something accomplished with your mouth.

I'm too modest to be modest.

If you steal, steal enough for a bribe.

A swelled lip stops a swelled head.

History was made to be changed.

Start the day off with a smile for breakfast and you will be hungry by lunch.

Do you think the only time to have an idea is now? I think so.

The past was yesterday, the present is today, the future is tomorrow, don't live in the past, and get ready for the future today.

Sometimes the brave person knows the game is fixed. (Two meanings)

I believe in hard work, the more I work, the more work I find, if you believe in doing nothing, the more nothing you will find.

Anonymous; who cares?

Behind every great woman there's a great woman.

If you can't say something good about someone, you are probably right.

I don't give a damn what a beaver does, it's the bear or the bull I'm worried about.

One minute with someone may be worth a year with another.

Less than one person in a million is truly famous, and I feel like one in a million.

To reply to silence with silence can kill a conversation.

It's a hick town of only two houses, the mayor lives in one, and the other house is vacant.

Not all prisons hold criminals, and some prisons are in our heads.

Ignorance is silence spoken to soon.

Time travel happens every night to me; I close my eyes at night, and I wake up in the future.

All parents are amateurs.

Everything has a first time.

The art of silence is my great reply.

We change only enough to be satisfied.

Keeping up with the Jones's is a Jones on your back.

The trouble with being rich is it costs too much.

Is there such a thing as a small crowd?

Hear no evil, speak no evil, see no evil, two out of three ain't bad.

It's funny, but humor is what you think it is.

A snail is faster than a nail.

Do Christmas presents make Christmas? Or does Christ make Christmas? If you don't know a bible would be a good Christmas present.

If you spend a long time convincing yourself, you'll never convince others.

Finding a dentist who will take payments is like pulling teeth.

Real power is the unseen puppet master and not the puppet.

It's no longer majority rules, but the squeaky wheel that gets the rule.

A coward has a silent complaint.

I can't make you change your personality or your nationality.

I have the best conversations when I'm by myself.

If you think you can't do anything about your circumstances you are right.

I wish, I wish, I wish, I wish I had a wish.

I should be fired, but my boss doesn't do his job.

A job is buying a slave for 8 hours.

I have been lead, and now I lead, I follow myself.

Every gain has a small loss and every loss has a small gain.

I feel like a kid on my 60th birthday, or did I just kid myself?

Discipline yourself to discipline yourself.

I work long and hard so I won't have to work later, I just don't work on making later sooner.

Young and smart makes old and smart.

Too much stuff becomes too much junk.

You never have appreciated your job so much until they tell you you're fired.

Too many cooks need to be laid off.

Indecision is a civil war in your mind.

WHAT IS THE MEANING OF LIFE? To live!

I taught a bully a lesson one time, and that was how to stop a nose from bleeding.

Silence it's sometimes best unsaid.

If you can't stand the heat, try not to go to hell.

You get out of life what you think into it.

Two rights don't make a wrong, but four rights may get you back to where you started from.

What to buy for the man that has everything? Shelves.

Flying is when you spend more time in the airport than in the air.

There are two sides to every story, my side and the wrong side.

The reward for honesty doesn't pay much, the reward for dishonesty is 5 to 10.

Indecision is when you decide not to decide.

The man that tells you everything is hiding something.

History can be repeated and rewritten. History can be repeated and written.

To the person that has something to say about everything, shut up.

To the ugly girl that thinks she's pretty, you are pretty ugly.

There is such a thing as an honest thief, but I never know what I'm talking about.

Silence is knowing when to speak.

The mouth is faster than the action.

Words won't fix the fence. (Double meaning)

The rich in first class,
The middle class in middle class,
The poor in third class,
But any class can have no class.

A fire place is good for heat; a house on fire is not.

Words echo from your mouth that may come back to your ears later.

Try to live life two days at a time, if you can't just live today.

Look first then leap, the seat may be up?

Sometimes an excuse is handy, and sometimes a handicap.

The wonderer drifts, I wonder why?

What is, is, what ain't ain't, if it is ain't it?

The future is yet to be, the past is the past, and if you're living in the past you have no future.

A good quote echoes back, I repeat, a good quote echoes back.

The meek try to obey the law, the powerful misuse the law, that's the law of nature.

A psychic reading is something only a psycho would believe.

If you point your finger then look in a mirror.

It's my style to be in style.

Health care is killing me.

They gossip in hell.

I don't consider that I am getting older; I am just getting closer to the finish line.

Trust a thief and learn a lesson.

If the Devil can't do it he will send a woman to do it.

I don't like to be average and that is what makes me average.

The person that takes his job to bed rests not.

Quantity is quick and questionable, but quality always qualifies.

My mother was in labor for 24 hours, and then she quit her job.

She was talking about her weight on the stairs; she said she was going down as she was going up.

It seems I live life one step forward and two steps backwards, maybe I should change direction?

Stand tall and be willing to back your backbone up.

For those who do not agree with my opinions, you should not be killed, just imprisoned long enough for you to change your mind.

Evil seeks the mind first, the heart second, and others third.

It is my opinion that you are opinionated.

Most obstacles in life are self made.

I have no complaints except for that I have nothing to complain about.

Too late is late, can you relate.

Let and old argument stay old.

The sure thing blinds you to the obstacles in the way.

The mouth can often fight better than the fist.

A mule is another name for an ass, and my mother-in-law is a real mule.

If you think there are two sides to every story, then you are missing a side.

Illusion is a delusion.

Never forget your roots, mine are gray.

Immortality I'm dying to get it.

Unforgivable becomes unforgettable.

It was the sleep part of the speech that I liked best.

To die in the theater is part of life in the theater.

Tragedy is the mind that thinks of tragedy.

I bought a memory course, and I can't remember where I put it.

I had a verbal contract on paper.

Inspiration makes perspiration.

Variety is the spice of life, blonds, brunets and red heads.

One door closes a better one opens.

Your mouth is where trouble is stored.

Paradox sign- "Everything $1.00 each"

If you don't know ask, and if they don't know, I would make something up.

To let others think for you I think is wrong.

To take advantage of disadvantage is not to your advantage.

Be glad that you can be glad.

I don't care about envy, I only care that you have more than me.

I'm not dumb; it's that everybody else is just too smart.

Since I turned 50 the world has gotten much older.

If the same old same old is getting old, quit doing the same old same old.

The best laid plans of mice and men are to plan that some will be mice and some will be men.

To change your weight you must first change your mind.

They'll never replace the horse, said Mr. ED.

I rest when I get home, I rest on the weekends, I rest in bed, I don't want to work, and I rest my case.

Become a businessman and keep your business to yourself.

You can find a lot of change with your head down, and you can see a lot of birds with your head up, either way you may get hit by a car.

Home is a great place to visit but I won't want to live there.

If you fight the future you will live in the past.

I have the keys to the city, now all I have to do is find the door.

It's the low man on the totem pole that often gets the most weight on him.

If you live in the past, then life has passed you by.

To gain strength, add more weights, in all areas of life.

Don't look back with envy, look ahead with envy.

Cowards may turn courageous after the crowd leaves.

Evil is live spelled backwards.

History stutters.

Timing is everything and its later then you think.

The letters in the word ALPHABET are not in alphabetical order.

A job is a form of slavery, and overtime is voluntary slavery.

Gossip is when the mouth won't kill what the ear hears.

Gossip is a tag game of words.

Fast food fat stomach.

Watch your weight because others are watching.

The same with the same keeps you sane.

Conflict of interest, a doctor makes more money when you're sick.

Tongues hang out together.

Something for nothing is something I often can't afford.

The gates of hell await the one who raises hell.

Good advice is often just telling someone what they already know.

The consequence of being right is that you might be wrong.

The rich have better taste in equality than the poor.

Study the past to study the future.

Don't believe every bad thing people say about you, even though they are true.

Equality is when you both know you're better than the other.

Babies make babies out of adults.

Imagination or action, most choose imagination, imagine what would happen if they choose action?

You can only change your future.

If you excel my faults I shall excel my fist.

Think first speak second.

Forgive and forget, don't forget to forgive.

Come and walk alone with me.

My Dear Frenchmen,
There is a difference between nonviolence and surrender.
Thank You,
USA

If I want a good conversation I'll talk to myself, if I want to be crazy I'll talk back to myself, if you want to talk to me stand in line.

One way to have peace on earth is for everyone to move to another planet.

If you believe that all things are possible then they are.

I swim better than a rock, because eventually I will come to the top.

The best things in life are free and freedom.

To the newly graduated, Mc Donald's is hiring.

Don't take an aspirin if you can get rid of what is giving you the headache.

The best way you can help anybody is to help yourself first.

Hang around with crooks and they will steal your reputation.

Your tongue is the reason why the knife is in your back.

If you want to please someone agree with him.

The weatherman says rain so I packed my picnic basket.

The universe is not larger than my imagination.

If you snub your nose at others, make sure you're not an other!

Time VS money, can money buy time, or can't time buy money?

I'll put up with anything that doesn't affect me.

Grey hair on a man makes him look distinguished, and grey hair on a woman make her look for a dye job.

I want sunny weather so I pray for rain.

I wore out many shovels and many shovels have worn me out.

Healthy, wealthy, and wise, if not complain.

He who desires not is undesirable.

Only people with laryngitis should be able to sing country.

Put my body in jail and my mind will tell me I'm on a beach, ain't life a beach.

A little done today is less to do tomorrow.

I'm not a bad actor; I was playing the part of a bad actor.

I'm now at the age that everyone says you look good for your age.

Time outlives all clocks.

You can't see it all, you can't know it all, but you can try to B.S. them all.

Bad plans swim like a rock.

Inability is the ability not to have ability.

Sometimes inaction is the best action.

Actions are the mirror for tomorrow.

The judge will judge your money first and you second.

Flattery will get you everywhere.

At one time thinking the world was round was crazy, and it seems like today the whole world is round.

Without the insane how would we know we are sane?

The noise of the city is the toys of the city.

I like ivory,
And I like oak,
I don't like poison oak,
Or poison ivory.

The past, the present and the future, you can only live in one of them.

Common sense, what's the sense in being common.

The seven deadly sins, I'm at 100%.

Can one have what one can't have?

Your strength is your lack of weakness.

Your words are like the wind it can't be seen or taken back.

I don't want what I threw out unless someone else wants it.

If you can't beat them join them- in hell.

If you have to tell someone how smart you are you're not.

If someone tells you how smart you are, be smart enough to check your wallet.

If you tell everyone how smart you are, make sure your hat fits on your swelled head.

Once time passes you can't get it back, good news, there's more time coming.

Some people have a hard time turning 50, and others do not, I guess it's a 50/50 chance.

To be really good at deception you must first deceive yourself.

Silence can't be heard only listened to.

I keep my own ideas; I don't want anyone else's ideas, because they may be judgmental?

If you think about what you are thinking, you may change your mind.

The best is yet to come, I hope so, I'm getting older and I haven't seen it.

Imagine that you have no imagination.

Every dream has an alarm clock.

You can change your mind but not the weather, and sometimes the weather can change your mind.

I am the captain of my destiny,
I do not abandon the ship in hard times,
But, I do have sense enough not to go down with the ship.

A working hand holds a hand full of money, and a lazy hand needs a hand out.

To those who think they are above the law, you must have money.

Help yourself to knowledge, happiness, envy, fear, fun or nothing, but it is you who must help yourself.

I'm not against free speech; I'm against people speaking opinions that are opposite of mine.

Lawyers and leaches.

Changing your mind is like changing your underwear; women do it more than men.

The wrong answer is not the answer.

Time is both changeable and unchangeable.

Haste is the long path.

The only bad thing about losing is you didn't win.

Good gossip may leave a sliver in the ear.

A quick hello and a quick good-bye, makes a great conversation.

I have but three complaints in life, the first is that I was born; the second is that I'm living; the third is that I must die.

If you don't consult me you insult me.

I act like a spring chicken at the bottom of a hill, and I act like a fried chicken at the top.

You only have to make it to old age once.

When you do step two before step one you will fall.

I'm not turning 50; it's my 30th anniversary of me turning 20.

I set my example in silence.

Life is the best teacher.

Gossip is based on 50% truth and 50% of what I want it to be the truth.

The sound of running water on a rock beats the sounds of a ticking clock.

Feel pity for others and never feel self-pity.

The peace maker has the bigger stick.

O' yesterday, O' yesterday,
O' why did I wish for today?
O' today, O' today,
I wish today would go away,
O' tomorrow, O' tomorrow,

Get me out of today,
O' will I wish my life away?

From the tongue comes compliment or curse.

I'm too honest to be dishonest,
I'm too respectful to be disrespectful,
I'm too interesting to be disinteresting,
I'm too graceful to be a disgrace,
I'm too illusioned that I'm disillusioned.

Friend or foe, one will try to hurt you and the other will try to borrow money.

If we kill all the lawyers, then who will write their wills?

Ugly is in the eye of the beholder.

Indecision makes for a bad decision.

Easy come easy go, hard come easy go.

Work to live, not live to work.

Home is home, work is work, please know the difference.

I was not hot until you said you were,
I was not hungry until you said you were,
I was not broke until you said you needed a loan.

Life is like insanity; don't think you can figure it out.

Statistics have many ways to be written.

Statistics can statistically make them say anything.

The unnatural with practice becomes natural.

A kid wears rose color glasses.

To better the world is to better yourself.

There's a chicken in every pot and a pot on every belly.

One weed brings company.

Opportunity and dishonesty are two different things.

I have news for you, the news you see is from the liberal's point of view, and that's the news.

I got some good news in the mail, I didn't get any mail.

Good lawyers let bad men go free.

Father time knows the right time for you to become a father.

It sometimes takes more work to get out of the work than the actual work would have taken.

The best thing about living your dreams is there are no commercials.

To the child in you, keep up the good work.

Time changes everything including time.

Money is a disease, both having it and not having it.

Everyone has a story and only the famous people have their's told.

Sometimes I wish I didn't get what I wished for.

The man at peace is the man at sleep.

It's you and I against the world, and I'm on break.

Don't worry about worrying; it's as simple as that.

Liberals follow a sinful view point and are told it's not sin; they follow this view point to hell, so say to hell with liberals.

A coward must live with himself, even if he's afraid of himself.

Silence can be more powerful than words.

We are on the team that could be champions, if the other teams weren't so good.

Mankind is not very kind.

Appreciate the things that you have and you will have more than you think.

Children, I can take them or leave them at the orphanage.

Reasonable can be unreasonable at times; at other times unreasonable can be reasonable.

Fast start slow finish.

My week days consisted of 8 hours of work, 8 hours of sleep, and 8 hours of work.

Can you fall asleep during a wake?

My sister went to college for a bachelor, but all of the men were married.

Dwarfs are in small demand today.

You can't play dirty without getting dirty.

If steel stocks are down they may be a steal.

The outcome of an idiot with income is maybe he's not such an idiot?

If all of greed was put into a bag, and everyone could take some, would many people take more than their fair share?

I saw David Copperfield, and he wasn't anything like the book.

From coward to courageous is often just how the story is told.

If someone makes you angry then there are two people with a problem.

You don't have to eat beans to be a stinker.

Timing is everything, and there is a time for everything, what are you doing with your everything?

I am for sale and my paycheck is the bill of sale.

A person that talks negative will run your positive down.

Don't confuse my hardhead with my strong will.

Every employee is someone selling their time for money, and money can't buy time.

The shortest distance between two points is to ask for directions first.

Stress is your mind in distress.

Stress is like a headache it's all in your mind.

Who are they? They say do this, they say do that, they say, I wish they would keep out of my business.

The word please and a smile will take you many miles.

A stranger is on probation for a few minutes.

If you misunderstand a mistake could it then be right?

Honor over riches makes you rich.

The only person that has fooled me several times is me.

The wicked man is his own worst enemy.

Exercise your body, exercise your mind, and exercise your rights.

I don't contradict myself, I just lie to myself.

Children are children and grandchildren are grand children.

Daydreams are what gets us through the day.

Sometimes it's not what you pay for it's what you don't pay for.

If wishes were fishes we would all wish for beef.

Know the difference between biting your tongue and swallowing your pride!

Even a man with dyslexia knows right from wrong.

I am what I am and I am hard to change.

If you can't afford to advertize you can't afford to stay open, this message brought to you by the ad counsel.

The more my greed the more I need.

If you are smoking and drinking change your stinking thinking.

If you think it can't happen to you, just keep living.

I'm growing.
I'm grown,
I'm growing older,
I'm grown old,
I'm growing daisies.

Leave your troubles at the door and you will snore.

Take your own advice about worry and don't.

Someone with a soft skull can have a hardhead.

I don't know why no one invites me to their parties, I tell such great stories.

The lawyer makes the insignificant significant.

One thing learned by experience is worth two things learned from a book.

More is an addiction.

It takes forceful to beat force.

Little + Little = Much.

For Christmas I would like a gift certificate good at any store- called cash.

If matter and anti-matter meet, does it matter?

Lead is so heavy that a pound of it weighs 2 pounds.

If it looks like Satan, talks like Satan, and acts like Satan, it might be a liberal.

Satan and liberals speak with the same tongue.

Minority + Majority = 100%

When right is wrong and wrong is right is it right?

It is not my fault that I have no faults.

If you wear the label of liberal you are lacking in logic.

The stimulus package is a temporary bandage on a permanent wound.

The hate crime bill gives liberals a license to hate.

The hate crime bill hates, and I hate this bill.

Self-esteem I'm not good enough to have it.

A violent mouth leads to a distribution of a fist.

The young try to change the world and the world tries to change the young.

There's bravery in numbers.

It takes two to argue and one to get along.

In life we do or we do without.

If it's free, watch out.

If it's free it costs.

If I say I'll sell it cheap, I mean I'm selling junk.

Your mind can be like a prison, the only escape plan is to talk to the warden.

I was not taking a nap; I was just finishing my night's sleep.

They need to open more left handed stores, right.

One man can't take on the whole world, and sometimes the whole world can't take on one man.

A survey was done on people who LIE, but the results were unreLIEable.

Your character is what you are, your reputation is what you do, and they always match.

An imagined evil can be worse than the real thing.

Are you aware that by using only 3% of your brain that it's hard to be aware.

We would all be great if the word if weren't in our way.

A good attitude is gratitude.

Offenders often see no crime.

Haste makes you last in the race.

Wicked ways worry.

The loud mouth never gets the short end of the stick.

If you are worried about getting a good night's sleep, you won't.

When you shoot your mouth off, someone may ask you to put your money where your mouth is, but you may already have your foot in your mouth.

If someone is afraid of the dark they will slow up, don't let ignorance be your dark.

If you dance every day that means you are not dead.

You don't judge others until you judge yourself, and if your honest you will stop judging others.

The old move like a snail and the dead move like a nail.

In God we trust on U.S. money, God was kicked out of the schools, the court system, so how much could this money be worth?

Beauty is skin deep, and when you have it you wear it on the outside.

The government is my imaginary friend.

I have two enemies the devil and myself.

I am just a dream of my dream.

It is possible that possibilities are possible.

It is possible that the impossible is possible?

When you are young and fall off a horse, you may break something, when you're my age you know not to get on the horse.

A rocking chair goes nowhere but moves, don't pattern your life after one.

A good leader should be a good greeter.

Most people down than up. (There are 3 meaning to this statement)

To find out how far you can go, find out how far you won't go.

If you put your foot in your mouth, what makes you think if you open your mouth again that you can get your foot out?

You are worthy of being worthy?

Which came first the apple or the apple seed?

If you steal a pig or a penny, you're still a thief.

Build your life on being honest and they will remember what you have done, build you life on being dishonest and they will remember what you have done.

A brief point made is remembered, a long speech is forgotten.

I prophesize that I can't see into the future.

If you had a pair of pears, how many pears would you have? 2 or 4 or more?

To wait causes aggravation, I try to wait before I get aggravated.

One if by land, two if by sea, I'd rather take a number one on land than a number two on the sea.

The best defense is not to do the crime.

If a man steals a loaf of bread to eat- so be it, if a man steals steak to eat he has ambition.

I used my visa to get out of the country, and my master card to get back in.

If you are window shopping at a jewelry store, make sure you don't buy glass?

It's not that I wasn't paying attention; it's just that I didn't care.

They say weed makes you forget things, someone asked me if I smoke weed and I said no, then I thought about it and maybe I forgot that I did?

The more beautiful the girl is, the looser the wallet is.

Exercise your right to exercise.

Magic won't fix the budget.

Listen, think, and speak.

Bide your time, the moment will soon be here; pay day!

Say what you mean and mean what you say, that's what I say and I mean it.

Minimum wage,
Minimum skills,
No thrills.

Don't make a lot,
Don't do a lot,
Don't have a lot,
But want a lot.

Seeing is believing, and believing in what you can't see is the trick.

The beggar often has more money than you.

Today is yesterdays tomorrow.

Due to circumstances beyond my control I can't make you listen to me.

If the weather man was a little better I wouldn't be looking at the weather girl. (Three meanings to this)

The rest of your life starts NOW!

I'm not needy I'm greedy.

Healthy, wealthy and why not?

Yesterday I said tomorrow would never come, and I was right.

In your mind if you don't mind, your mind doesn't mind, and if your mind does mind then it matters, maybe I should just mind my own business.

The tongue has no mind.

I dare you to cross the line, and if you do, I dare you to jump off a cliff.

Power is addicting.

If you don't lie to yourself you won't lie to others.

Take time to sharpen an axe and it comes back 10 fold.

All parents are amateurs.

The art of silence is my great reply.

A hardheaded person has a hard time accepting that he has a hard head.

What is the meaning of life? The answer is to live!

Silence it's sometimes best left unsaid.

Silence is best appreciated after two loud mouths talk.

If more is less, the more things change the less they change?

More is less and free is expensive.

Let your smile be your sunshine, but take your umbrella.

Fame comes with flame. (Candle flame from working late)

E=MC Squared and I don't care.

If you love the past you may live in hell in the future!

Socialism, Darwinism, atheism, terrorism, communism, they all can go to HELLisum.

I only have two problems with my job, the work and the workers.

To live on easy street you may have to put many people on skid row.

I'm working overtime on the couch tonight.

The only thing I can't stand is standing.

Never send a man to do a woman's work.

A know it all has to tell it all.

If you're right, you're right, if you're wrong, it wasn't you.

An echo is a form of gossip, do you have an echo?

Overconfident undertrained.

With or without perfume bologna is still bologna.

If you want your opinion to be right make sure it matches mine.

In scrabble a word can be made up, and the bluff called, and then you can disinrobbate them.

Perhaps a man has nothing to say because he hears nothing worth commenting on.

Inside a fat man there is a smaller hungry man.

If you tell it like it is, make sure you know what it is.

Silence can be a better weapon than a gun, just don't tell anyone.

Believe it, achieve it, and receive it.

It's hard to buy a car without a job, and hard to get a job without a car.

If you can't laugh at yourself, other people may laugh at you.

The meaning of life is to please both God and yourself.

Over the years I have learned to trust in myself and listen to myself, the trouble with this is I give bad advice.

It cost a buck to drop a dime.

I would volunteer for charity work, but I first have to talk to my lawyer about this.

Often to make a dream come true you must go through a nightmare.

The pill will kill, the herb is superb.

If you want to agree about disagreeing, that's fine, but you are still wrong.

We have ways of making a man talk; I just wish we had ways of making a woman shut up.

Officer the sign said "WET FLOOR" so I did.

Good food is good for the digestion, and bad food is good for indigestion.

I am jealous, I am greedy, but I am not jealous of my greed.

I am so lonely that I have loneliness to keep me company.

Without balance you will soon fall.

We change over time, even if we don't take time out to change.

The man that I like best I haven't met.

Ignorance is silence spoken to soon.

Man on a horse,
Man on a bike,
Both sit on their butts for exercise,
Man on a couch,
Man on a chair,
Because they just don't care.

Silence can be a pause that makes you think if the pause should be permanent?

I eat at a fine restaurant and I feel like a king,
I pay a tax to eat out,
I am the customer- the KING,
The tax is for the luxury of eating out,
The king should not have to clean up after himself,
But I do at burger king.

Two blind men will soon fall in a ditch, and these two liberals I hope can get out of the ditch. (Note one does not have to be blind to be blind)

Don't let a thief steal your honesty.

To reply to silence with silence can kill the conversation.

To blow your nose with just your fingers is snot easy.

On a diet, want to try it, killed the diet.

Poverty somehow only applies to the poor.

Poverty and poor, money poor, job poor, credit poor, when it rains it poor's.

If your enemy flatters you, check your wallet.

If you think the world revolves around you, then it must revolve around both of us?

Everyone was younger yesterday.

Dr Will prescribed a pill for a chill and gave me a bill.

All men are created equal, after a short time of being equal some become bettered equaled.

I had termites, so I got some carpenter ants to repair the damage.

I have quit only when I think I have quit.

In my mind I'm on vacation, in reality I'm at work.

To hear gossip at the business where you work is just business as usual.

A diary is a form of a time capsule.

Memory is just a diary in your mind.

The inventor is when an idiot becomes a genius.

Beauty makes ignorance attractive.

Common sense is what the common person does not have.

Stupidity repeats, stupidity repeats.

I was the oxymoron.

Beauty is the blinders of life.

Often the best help you can give someone is not to help them.

Nonsense makes no sense.

Insecurity kills security.

If I said you had a fat face it would go to your head.

Shoplifters get a 100% discount.

I shoplifted once and got caught, and I'll never do that again, get caught.

I'm probably not as modest as I think, I'm probably more so.

Life is like a classroom, you are the teacher and everyday you get a lesson, but for the wrong test.

I tried shoplifting once, but the shop was too heavy.

The man with back bone doesn't get his back broken.

Don't live in the past,
Don't live for today,
Don't live for the future,
Just live.

Forgiveness first, revenge second, if it were the other way around would I need forgiveness?

Imagination is the lie that gives motivation.

I wish the jail bird would become extinct.

Light pockets make a pick pocket pick a different pocket.

Few words make you think more than many.

One secret to life is simply to cope with all of the things you can't cope with.

When you are going to diet, don't wait to change your weight.

The man that runs his mouth will always go further than you, and if you don't believe me ask him.

There is enough room at the top to make the top the bottom.

Imagination is the only thing that makes me king.

It is not necessary to be necessary.

Rome wasn't built in a day; I think it took 3 weeks?

I think pot should be legal, because frying pans are.

From sane to insane is just an opinion.

The pick pocket also has pockets.

Silence is the friend of the man with no answer.

Opportunity is often something that looks like an obstacle.

Time travel, if you want to live in the future today, you can just do everything you would do tomorrow today.

A coward may be a lion from a far.

If you are in a hurry take time to ask for directions, or you will be going nowhere in a hurry.

Old age, start young, and then wait.

Two men had a dream, one man said I'll drink to that and the other lived his dream.

Punishment is a type of correction, so correct me if I'm wrong.

Sticks and stones may break my bones, but testimony can put you in prison.

If you can't find a job start your own business, I won't tell you how to do this because I want to stay out of your business.

I see clear vision of the year 2020 (Twenty, twenty).

A walk in the rain makes you appreciate your roof.

Mankind is kind of a smart fool.

If the obvious isn't the answer, obviously it's the wrong obvious.

The improbable is probably probable.

If you don't know the meaning of the word quit, buy a dictionary.

Judge a man by his works and not by the works of his mouth.

If you can't dance and you can't sing, get into show business.

A young boxer doesn't know the ropes.

True peace is having a piece of mind.

Fat is like credit, easy to get and hard to get rid of.

The parents that raise their kids well can sleep well.

Two half truths don't make one truth.

New Japanese saying "Made in China."

A tattoo is the signature of immaturity.

Inch by inch makes a mile.

90% pain brings 10% gain.

Civilization has the death penalty, what's civilized about that?

Most people that don't know what they want in life don't know what they want after life.

I'd rather live 90 years well than 100 years of hell.

You can't pay some people to get a job.

Most people change their age before they change their opinion.

Does it matter which way you go if you have no direction?

It's not that I'm so smart; it's that everyone else is so dumb.

Life is like a chess game, you keep making your best move until it's over.

Liberals happen.

I love my job on the weekends.

I am? I think?

Life is like an enema, do I need to say more.

There are more honest then dishonest, but dishonest makes the press, honest.

I wear a birthday suit on a nudist beach.

Mexico is located near the bottom of the top.

Two words that I hate most are ain't.

What can be spoken can be broken.

Retirement is the end of slavery.

How does the world run? The elected tell the journalists half truths, and the journalist tells us half lies.

The story changes with the story.

Weeds come and weeds go,
Oh- how they grow,
Why can't a flower grow like a weed?
I guess it's all in the seed.

F.D.R. J.F.K. L.B.J. R.I.P.

Useless now may be useful later.

Are most of us anonymous narcissist?

I believe you can have disbelief.

In the court system innocence is if you have enough money or not.

Slavery is over, so back to work I go.

A man with a one track mind can be hit by a train.

One thief they hung low,
One thief they hung high,
One thief they let go,
Because he let go of some of the money he didn't own.

Show mercy to a criminal and you will have to show it twice.

Jail birds of a feather flock together.

The evening news treats its viewers like Pavlov dogs, but I trained myself when they ring the bell I change the channel.

Envy is the ball and chain worn in one's mind.

A blind man needs a light bulb only for guests.

To wear a welcome out once is to wear it out for life.

A hard day's work or a hard day of relaxation, both have 24 hours.

Hope is a lie that helps us get through another day.

I work hard at doing nothing.

Reasons change over the seasons.

Often there is no gain when having too much.

Anything first starts in your mind.

Oh how can I have so much wit?
Oh how can I have so much wisdom?
Oh how can I look so good?
Oh how can I be so modest?

To answer or not to answer, for that is the question?

Imagination is just something thought of in your mind.

If you only learn what you want to, you won't earn what you want to.

If the question is complicated simplify the answer.

I have one thing that I know for a fact, and that is that there are no facts.

We want what we can't get and we get what we can't want.

One thing about inconstancy is that over time it is constant.

In an argument, you don't give up until you shut up.

Enjoyment is a form of wealth that money can't buy.

If you are going to worry, worry about how much joy you have.

It was the woman that made me sin, she made me drink, miss work and do anything else that I just feel like doing.

Civilization is rarely civilized.

The news is a form of gossip.

The rich man has ice in the summer; the poor man has melted ice in the summer.

The tide makes no difference to a sunken ship.

Our country has changed with the times, from Godly to ungodly.

I am the only one that can save me from myself.

A rose pleases your eye, and the thorns are not noticed.

Busy without direction is busier.

What happens happens, but make a plan for the happen to happen in your favor.

Genius, it's all in your mind.

You don't need an excuse if you do nothing wrong.

If you have received a compliment, then check your pocket.

I gossip not when I'm asleep.

Guilty by reputation is not a good thing, but a true thing.

Have the devil for company and he will always overstay his welcome.

I am a victim of my own mind.

An amateur knows 90% of the job, and is 90% cheaper.

Take responsibility for your own actions instead of your act.

I have good news, there is no news.

Have money, have meal.

I am the hero of my mind.

Gravity if it were worth anything it would be sold by the pound.

An enema to my enemy.

It's not always better to work, work, work; sometimes it's just better to work.

Too much equality said the midget to the giant.

All men are created equal, the giant believes it, and the midget doesn't.

In life you can take the long road or the short road, most take the short road, but most of the time the short road turns out to be the long road.

Keep your dreams alive, stay asleep.

A job is a career gone wrong.

The reason our company can't get anything done is because we have a boss.

The boss asks me for suggestions and doesn't use them, and I suggest he stops asking me.

The busy bee is trying not to be a want to be.

The more you gossip the easier it gets, that's what I heard.

Give the metric system an inch and it will take a meter.

The all mighty buck can buy an all mighty buck (Deer).

There is less to magic than meets the eye.

You work work, don't let the work work you.

The future belongs to those who wait, but don't wait your future away.

My dreams are good for me and not you, and if you knew any better my dreams would be good for you.

The person that takes his job home with him doesn't get overtime for it.

A mother's baby is never ugly.

Rain is welcome on a hot day and snow not welcome on a cold day.

To stop learning is a start towards ignorance.

The hardhead is too much genius to change his mind, and to ingenious to conceive his hardhead.

I just turned 40 ten years ago.

At times a stubborn man is like a mule, and at other times he's like an ass.

Sometimes your family talks about your friends, and sometimes your friends talk about your family, they are usually both telling the truth.

You can't swallow your pride with your foot in your mouth.

If you are rich in greed, you will never be rich.

All work and no jokes lead to a stroke.

I have stupid parents and history repeats.

A good guest knows when to leave, and a better guest knows not to stay.

A little man jests and jokes to keep the king off his throat.

We all have the same stories.

Inflation is when more is less.

When bad is represented as good and good as bad, this is a bad thing, or do I mean a good thing?

It's hard to do better by trying, and easy to do worse without trying.

My advice to you is not to take any advice from anyone.

Some of us live life, molding it, shaping it, and others let life live them, molding them and shaping them.

Observation is best done with your mouth shut.

The mouth speaks wrongly,
The mouth eats too much,
The mouth smokes cigarettes,
The mouth makes a good scapegoat for the brain.

One word to describe me would be smart and modest.

It rains gold in the desert.

Both wealth and being poor have advantages, I like to take advantage of being wealthy.

I must enslave my thoughts before my thoughts enslave me.

Don't bring your problems home, there's a post office on the way home.

I'm not perfect, and I like everyone equally who is not perfect.

Many drops of water make up the ocean.

Buy high; sell low, the story of my life.

If it's deep in your mind, then bring your mind to your mouth.

Don't live in the past even if the rent was less.

When there's no hope, think that there is hope, and that should give you some hope.

A long speech makes for a long sleep.

Silence can say a whole lot.

If everyone knew civilization would end next month, civilization would end this month.

I hear gossip all around me, and I know who started it, I'll tell you, but don't tell anyone.

If you look back in anger you walk into a wall.

A birthday is a good time to begin anew, even though you are older.

The British are coming, said the prostitute.

Learn to be poor and practice to be rich.

From young to old is the person that thinks it.

The U.S. thinks it's the police of the world, and rest of the world thinks that the police are crooked.

If you can't stand it when morality has the upper hand, you will hate eternity.

Attack first, defend second, step three if needed- run!

Split personalities make for some good conversations.

If you want to look younger and you are 40 and look 50, just say you're 60.

Judge me by my actions, not by the gossip.

A laugh a day helps keep suicide away.

Great times make great men, and great men make the great times.

To sculpture hard marble is hard, to teach someone with a hardhead is harder.

A penny for your thoughts and I want my change.

I never met an Eskimo that liked snow, I don't like snow, and I never met an Eskimo.

A better tomorrow starts with a better today.

It's not only those with a hard head that can be hardheaded.

I tried and I tried, I tried everything but giving up.

If a man is willing to sell himself that's one thing, unwillingly is another.

The men who rewrite history must do it before judgment day.

The key to open a door is please.

Moderation it's only mediocre.

I literally think liberals are illiterate.

I have learned how to save myself from me, and you must learn how to save yourself from you.

Liberals live lies.

Old age, I think I'll just put it off for another year said the 100 year young man.

Evil grows.

Paycheck, it works for me.

I count sheep to get to sleep, and it works every time, so far 1,233 sheep and counting.

Think in 3D, thinking, planning, and doing.

I don't watch the news because it's a repeat.

Legal duress is a judge's decision.

Unrestrained power needs restraints.

Did you hear about the man that got hit by a train? There's one less liberal now.

Judge each day by the things you do, then judge the things you do.

I'll pick it up later, I'm not a slob, and a slob won't pick it up later.

Hot in the pot beats frozen in the freezer.

A nag a day keeps the hag away.

Publicity- it's all how you package it.

Do on to others as you would have others do on to you, capital punishment.

Live while you can before you kick the can.

Glad to see you, glad to see you go.

You learn more my listening than talking, so let me talk and you listen.

Trim the fat and you trim your fat.

It is easy for me to judge what I have not done.

For every successful man there's a mother.

If you can't climb a tree, then buy the fruit.

I do not lack ability, I just lack.

Imagine no imagination.

The weapons of mass destruction are the mouths and actions of the liberals.

An apple a day keeps the doctor away, and so will no insurance.

If it looks easy try it, it's not.

Live well, what good is it not to live well, well spoken.

Doubt a man that doubts himself, unless it's you.

Self-contradictory is a one word paradox.

Two cowards don't make one brave man.

Prisons are for criminals, and not to speak your mind is criminal.

Retirement is 7 Saturdays a week.

The best time to stand up for yourself is before someone knocks you down.

Many common men who emulate great men are one day likely to make great men common.

If the boss worked one day at my job he would quit, boss-I need another sick day tomorrow can you fill in for me?

Hope changes as age changes.

Everyone likes a winner; it's when you learn to like the loser you win.

The fine art of propaganda is called the news.

Your mind can be your invisible enemy.

I expected the unexpected.

Conversation travels.

A watched watch moves slowly.

Ask and ye shall receive, if not use your credit card.

A know it all mouth is moving too fast to learn anything.

Don't forget to use your memory, if I remember correctly it's the best way to build memory.

Follow my example and you will be ample.

Willpower is power.

There is not an explanation that I can't make up.

Yesterday was tomorrow so do what you said you would do today.

We are all the same color with the lights off.

Compromise is often compromised sin.

It's not a new era; it's only a new era to us.

What's wrong? Everybody is complaining that's what's wrong.

Hard work is for suckers and those who weren't born rich.

Like it or not, the likes you will like and the not's not.

If you spend a long time convincing yourself that you did something right, you didn't.

From head to toe I feel no woe so now is the time to go.

Anxiety is part of society.

Exercise your body, exercise your abilities, exercise your mind, it will make you health, wealth and wise.

Retirement is having the seniority to have 52 week's vacation per year.

Originality is just a copy of something that originally was hidden.

Sometimes being disadvantaged is to your advantage.

If you accept it, you deserve it.

Many things can choke a man, but none like pride.

Thinking is just an exercise for the brain.

The public restroom at the stock market, only in an emergency will I do my business there.

Courage is staying on a job for 30 years to raise a family, and a coward also does the same thing.

A job is just a form of paid slavery.

Living off your wits makes for a good diet.

Pity the pitiful.

One apple off the tree is not missed.

It is illegal to burn money and still I smoke.

The know it all usually knows nothing.

There's nothing the loud mouth can't do except shut up.

The more complicated the answer you are looking for, the more complicated the answer you can't find.

The joke that is the funniest is the truest.

For just one dollar I'll let you agree with me.

I'm not selfish I'm greedy.

The government is my bully.

You can't get back the life you have lived, but you can live the life still left.

The blind man's dream might not be for him to see, but for everyone else to go blind.

The bottom line is the poor are still at the bottom.

The poor pour out their hearts.

Talk is cheap and that's one cheap loud mouth.

An ounce of prevention is worth 453.59237 grams of cure.

I can rationally reason that I must act irrationally with you.

It's never too late, until you become late.

The 7 deadly sins, 6 out of 7 ain't bad.

My kingdom for a horse or a tank of gas.

The better the gossip the quicker it spreads.

Paradox- Too tired to sleep.

If the know it all only knew.

Wash a car, double the price.

The only way to see the writing on the wall is to read between the lines.

Most gossip is based on the telephone game.

You are only old enough to get a tattoo when you think tattoos are juvenile.

In my mind I am king, in reality I wish I were dreaming.

You can't do wrong doing right.

I wish I could do half of the things today that I said I would do yesterday.

Everyone thinks differently don't you think?

Not all know it all's are conceited, take me for example.

Magic is the absence of logic.

Practice today makes perfect tomorrow.

Why do people with nothing to say, say?

Take time to smell the roses, because one day the roses may smell you.

Mind over mouth.

Time will tell said the diamond to the coal.

I'm not conceited, but I just hit my halo on the doorway.

Too much sleep makes you sleepy.

There is a type of order in disorder.

Time is money, and one day you will run out of money.

Tell my ears no secrets for my mouth talks.

My sword to the king and my money for me.

A hardheaded person has a hard way to go.

Don't be the ass sitting in first class, and say excuse me when I bump into you.

Electronics is the easy way to make your life harder.

Read a quote as a child and it means one thing, read the same quote as a young man and it means something else, read it as an old man and it reads as the truth.

All unions give us more, and the companies must raise their prices, now my money is worth less, now I need a raise.

There is an exception to every rule except this rule.

Idle hands volunteer too be idle.

Welfare- When it rains it POORS.

Enslave a man's mind and you won't have to enslave his body.

If a psychologist understands psychology, maybe he needs a psychologist?

I predict the future will come.

The photograph looks just like me, and that's why I don't like it.

The loudness of a neighbor can only be appreciated in the country.

The many as one, has only one drawback, and that's you can't get everyone to unite.

A hint in the art of observation, watch nothing more.

The loud mouth can talk while chocking on his words.

Don't worry about what's behind you, don't worry about what's in front of you, and just don't worry.

Slow and steady wins the race, I say at best 2nd place.

We can profit from a loss when we learn from a loss.

Live around lies and the truth is not believed.

The big mouth can get a fat lip to match.

Gossip gathers gossip.

A lazy life gets lazy rewards.

The squirrel cage in my mind spins faster when oiled with thought.

Nonviolence I'm not going to fight you over it.

We will always have the poor; thank God I don't have to be one of them.

Not everyone fears a tyrant, and not everyone is married to one.

A man climbs a mountain to find God, and maybe that man should be happy he didn't find him?

Too much practice makes for complacency.

The beginning is not always the best place to start.

The man that tells on himself has nothing left to hide.

Many weak men make up the world, and a few strong men shape it.

Finding faults with others is a fault in you.

I just wish I knew half of what I thought I knew when I was 17.

The fit have fun.

My desire is not to desire.

Imagination exaggerates.

Not all gossip needs repeating.

Hardheaded now is hardheaded later.

Standing up to a bully doesn't make you a bully.

The choice you make today is the decision you live with tomorrow.

If you think you can't you won't.

History is what I am doing at this moment.

A good reputation is built on hard work, and a bad reputation is built on hardly working.

Live life before life outlives you.

If you have all the answers to all the questions, then you should question the questions or the answers?

My clothes aren't out of style everyone else is out of the cycle.

Gossip has large ears.

If you play with fire, one day you will pray for rain.

A hole in the roof will soon put a hole in the floor.

Less is more, more or less.

Leisure is a waste of a good heart attack.

If you think you are dumb, you will be dumb, if you think you are smart, make sure you don't think you are too smart.

I envy what everyone else has, but not what I have.

Be grateful for bad luck, and good luck, until one day when your luck runs out on you.

Employment is just a form of slavery.

The truth about truth is that it is true.

A hero is the one who doesn't know it because this hero was too busy raising a family.

The difference between arrogance and being important is what other people think.

Planning for the best is much better than hoping for the best.

In our own minds we are all great.

Equality is the quality to seek.

If I have insulted you I'm sorry, and I'm sorry you are like that.

To the person that talks a good show, when it's time to show they usually don't show.

What straw broke the camel's back? And what straw will break your back?

Hardheaded closed minded.

Someone hit my car, they had no insurance, so they lied, I just wish they had some LIEability.

The naïve are easily lead and the average person is very naïve.

The news is one big staged show, and if they can conceive it don't you believe it.

The magic of the news is to get your attention here when the trick is going on there.

The news is a created show, with the idea of fooling a foolish audience, and the audience appreciates a good show.

The harder your head the harder you will fall.

A fast decision can make a slow way out.

If you let other people think for you, YOU may never think you are wrong.

Don't live too much of today for tomorrow.

Look at what you have and don't look at what you have not, for the blind look at nothing.

If you can't find time for direction now, you will need plenty of time to be lost later.

Some people live in the past every day, and that makes today still part of the past, they should get past this.

If you trust in yourself and others will trust in you.

If worse comes to worse, things might be the worstest.

Depression has much company when alone.

Company is not called talking to yourself, that's called a good conversation.

A good detective makes the insignificant; significant.

If you have to think, did I do the right thing, you didn't.

The devil made me do it, but God will punish me for it.

There is a difference between being crazy and being a comedian, and I just don't know what that difference is.

Every year I get older I expect less and I get what I expected.

Bad thoughts we do to ourselves.

Silence is golden so please be like gold.

Home is where the mortgage is.

I desire to act on my desires.

A ship needs an anchor so as not to drift, don't let your mind become an anchor.

If you choose someone for an enemy there is something wrong with you, if someone chooses you for an enemy there's something wrong with you.

I have patience for everything but tolerance.

If you assume long enough, I assume you will get a law suit.

The wicked use language to make wicked things seem good, always listen between the words.

The illusion of life knows there is no magic.

It's not too late to start a diet after the meal.

Short term things fall short.

It is unreasonable to think that reason would not work.

There is more to life than life.

There is a STORY in hiSTORY.

The poor are the last people on earth that should have any money, they would just spend it getting out of debt.

I have an abundance of nothing.

What good does positive thinking do?

The last 6 times I was wrong I was right 2 of those times.

I do great things in my mind all day long.

One bad apple can spoil the whole bunch, and the same is true with a bad friend.

The state of confusion is our largest state.

Ignorance of being ignorant is ignorant.

If you have to take the low road to get to the high road, is the trip worth it?

Learn from the past to build the future.

One ounce of troubles is 100 pounds of imagination.

I'm not crazy, the rest of the world is.

Unpredictability, after a while, can become predictable.

Fiction is counterfeit money.

Improve yourself today and show others tomorrow.

A thief must lock his property up; for he assumes that someone will steal it back.

Punishment, put them in jail, feed them, clothe them, no bills, no taxes, no responsibilities, what are we waiting for?

My weekend consists of 24 hours of sleep, 24 hours of T.V. and 24 hours of being nagged.

Smiles are contagious.

He's lazier than a Maytag repairman.

Silence is the ability to hold your job.

Greed is one thing that you hoard or don't.

I don't like the opera because I can't tell who is winning.

Be polite to others, it doesn't cost a thing, and may cost you if you don't. Thank you.

No man is an island, but a man can own an island.

A tarnished reputation does not shine.

The time machine- if you want time to slow down watch a clock, if you want time to speed up have a good time.

Nuclear weapons- When the lion roars, people tremble.

In faith I believe, and I believe in faith.

Oxymoron- Everyone loves to hate me.

A cheap apartment is a castle to a homeless person.

Silence won't make you put your foot in your mouth.

The stomach has a brain of its own.

The cycle of life from 1 to 11 years old copy your parents, from 12 to age 21 copy your friends, from age 22 to 49 be yourself, from age 50 and older become your parents.

Don't make fun of people, make fun of what they do.

Words can wound you long after a sword has rusted. (Two meanings)

One man with courage is worth a dozen cowards.

A hardhead will never convince himself that he's wrong, so you must argue with him until you become hardheaded.

Being hardheaded is not admitting you are wrong, I'm not hardheaded, but I'm never wrong.

Everyone has a hard head, but you don't have to be hardheaded.

Being a liberal is just a lack of knowledge, and no trouble speaking your lack of knowledge.

Being hardheaded is a con game the mind plays on us, and no one wants to admit being conned.

It doesn't take two people for one person to be hardheaded.

If you never lose your temper you can never lose everything that you have.

Injustice becomes justice when the money changes hands.

The poor eat bread; the rich make the bread so they can stay rich and can eat steaks.

Don't be afraid to be humble, it may save you a lot of being humbled later.

You are never too old to dream, just too tired to try it.

Imagine if there was no imagination.

If he's so famous how come he doesn't even know who I am?

Truth or false? (Please re-read)

If I had a boat I would call it champion, that way I would always have a championship.

Praise and belittlement can both last a lifetime.

Imagination is an illusion.

I like 90 degree weather until it gets here.

99% of my circumstances are made by me, and the other 47% is due to my lack of education which is also my fault.

If you are happy with 2nd place, you will wind up near last place.

I think I can imagine, therefore I can.

A hero stands on two legs and a coward runs on two legs.

The next time you can't sleep, imagine you are asleep.

Destiny is often by design.

Dignity is often just knowing when to shut your mouth.

Patience; I'm getting tired of it.

Practice makes perfect, so practice to be perfect.

You are wrong when you are right, when you have a wrong attitude about being right.

A well done job will be noticed by others, and so will a poorly done job.

I have ears that hear and you have a mouth that talks, I also have feet that walk.

A tattoo shows your I.Q.

A bullet to the head and your dead, so bite the bullet the next time you are going to shoot your mouth off.

MISTAKES***************************
(Written by Joseph Bonkowski)

You may like making a mistake better if you call it getting some experience, so get ready for plenty of experience.

You will never make another mistake if you just call them errors.

I am tired of making mistakes so I decided to hire someone to do things for me, and that was just another mistake.

A mistake can be a form of education.

A tattoo is a young person's mistake.

Learn from other people's mistakes, so you will make fewer mistakes, because you make enough of your own.

Some of us make the same mistake twice, both coming and going, they just didn't see it coming.

If we could relive our lives we would just make different mistakes.

The future holds the futures mistakes.

It took a great deal of planning to make the mistakes that I have made.

Good advice costs little; not using it costs more.

I used to make mistakes, then I went to college, and now I make miscalculations.

I told him he was dumber than a rock, and he told me a rock never made a mistake.

I go from failure to failure, I try and I try, I plan and I plan, I don't repeat the same mistakes, I don't repeat the same mistakes.

Doers make mistakes, and doing nothing is a mistake.

If you are always the victim in life, make sure you are not the victim of an excuse.

Perception as I see it is me not making a mistake.

Sometimes being too careful not to make a mistake is a mistake.

Hast makes mistakes.

To double your mistake is to not admit you made one.

To err is human; to cover it up is also human.

Curiosity makes many mistakes.

Everyone makes mistakes with the possible exception of the loud mouth.

A mistake can be a great teacher.

To see a mistake before it happens is called life experience and so is not seeing the mistake.

To err is human, then study them and make less err.

I will do nothing so I make no mistakes, except for the mistake of doing nothing.

The more mistakes you make, the more you should learn, if not I don't know what to tell a fool.

If I had known when I was younger all of my mistakes, I would have just made all new mistakes.

Time will come, age will come, and mistakes will come.

MODERN PHILOSOPHY**************
(Written by Joseph Bonkowski)

Great men don't watch T.V. they are on T.V.

God is not your T.V. set, but he can see what you are watching.

It is not good that man should be alone, so television was created.

Welfare, why work? Sounds fair to me.

No fortunes are made between the bed and the T.V.

Something for nothing, see welfare.

Welfare is the leech of society.

My leisure time is my T.V. time, my procrastination time is my T.V. time, my free time is my T.V. time and just when do you think I have time to look for a job?

To be on welfare is to be enslaved without doing any work.

12 hours of sleep, and 12 hours of T.V., makes for a well balanced day.

The more things I have to do the more T.V. I watch.

Join the loser of the month club, and the requirements are 6 hours of T.V. per day.

The wages of incompetence is minimum wage.

To those of you who waste their life's playing video games, game over.

Do you think the great depression could have been prevented if they had Prozac back then?

I dream about virtual reality.

Welfare is a form of retirement.

Bibles and T.V.'s both outnumber the people, and only one is used daily.

Success is less than 1% T.V.

We don't like to wait in a line, and it's a waste of valuable time, time that could be used watching reruns on T.V.

You can't do anything great by watching T.V. even if you get up on the commercials.

Look up in the sky, it's a bird, it's a plane, it's someone trying to pick your pocket.

People on welfare get a 100% discount on everything.

Give a man a fish and you start another form of welfare.

It won't be long before every U.S. dollar is made in China.

It takes 4 cents to make one U.S. dollar, and 3 cents to make it in China.

For every book that sits on a self, there are 6 T.V.'s on.

The computer is now part of life, let's not delete it.

A fool and his money open E-Mails.

The internet highway travels much faster than the interstate highway.

The computer is powerful, so let's not let the government unplug it.

I can't waste my life sleeping, I have T.V. to watch.

It's hard to find a job when unemployment pays so well.

It seems like everything I buy is written in Spanish, and made in china.

F.D.R. said "You have nothing to fear but fear itself." and the Germans.

MONEY**************************
(Written by Joseph Bonkowski)

Credit cards are a weapon of mass destruction.

The pursuit of money makes for good followers.

Money makes money, and credit makes credit.

Debt gives you credit, and the more credit you have the more credit you can get, the more credit you get the more in debt you get, you get what you pay for.

Paper money will burn in hell, but Gold won't burn in heaven.

Everyone plays tag with money and chases money until the tax man chases them, then the game turns to hide and seek.

My stocks are diversified, they all go down evenly.

I have a ton of money and not an ounce of dignity.

A good sale or discount fills the house with junk.

The cost of living makes inflation.

Debt is like quicksand, its best not to step in it.

The man that becomes the bank for others soon is in bankruptcy himself.

If you spend your pay before you get it, do you also do your work before it is given to you?

Everyone plans their way out of debt, but not in.

To make a million dollars on paper is the easiest million dollars you'll ever make.

It is in my best interest to pay cash.

No need; no greed.

Money can stop you from being a slave to your job, and give you a new job of being the security guard of your money.

Because I work overtime I can't hear the birds working overtime.

What is a man's first million dollars but something he has given up on?

Time is money, but money is not time, it's time to make some money.

The economy needs some economy helper.

The best way to build a nest egg is not to put all your eggs in one basket.

Money is printed on paper and faith.

If you try to spend money you don't have (credit), maybe that's why you don't have any money?

Pay your bills in full and be fulfilled.

If God made money then why isn't his picture on it?

The bank may be broke, but the banker is never broke.

I don't know if God made money; but, God please make some for me.

Money buys honey, and I'm a busy bee.

Don't pick wealth over health; it's not the wealthy choice.

Vacant apartment brings vacant money.

The banks get rich because it's in their best interest to make interest off your interest.

If everyone were rich, no one would be rich.

God made money is called Gold and Silver.

Money is printed in hell.

I'm too poor to have money.

Save your pennies it makes sense. (Cents)

Inflation is like my belly, each year it gets bigger and harder to stomach.

A lesson learned by the seat of the pants may stay with you, a lesson learned by the emptying of the wallet may repeat.

A slogan for the lottery, "A little money goes a long way."

A slogan for the lottery, "A little money in, a lot of money out."

Tried and true and no payment too! (Paying with cash)

I make money, I give money to God, I spend money, and I can't cut out the middle man.

A slogan for the lottery. "It takes money to make money."

Money makes civilization for sale.

Things cost more when you have more.

If at first you don't succeed, buy, buy again.

Overtime is just money overspent.

I would say I will be rich in two years, if not add two more.

Everyone makes a fortune a few dollars at a time, everyone also spends a fortune a few dollars at a time.

Inflation, brother can you spare a dollar?

Spend dollars and get back change, save the change and get dollars.

Money is blind.

I have more money by folding it in half.

We accept cash with proper I.D.

Gold coffins rarely go up.

To waste money, a rich man or a fool, or a rich man ready to become a fool.

Money brings new relatives.

The more money you make per hour the less you do.

Money = Equality for all.

Money comes and money goes, just try to pay your bills before the money goes.

Care for your money now and your money will care for you later.

Wholesale, it ain't worth the cost.

Priceless, how much less is it priced?

Spending money is often not knowing what you want but buying it anyway.

Poverty is not a crime, excepting poverty is criminal.

Spend your time wisely, and you will have time to spend your money.

A penny earned is a penny saved, so I'll throw my two cents in, because talk is cheap and money talks.

Some of us know how to make money, and the rest play the lottery.

My money advice is to edit your credit.

Poverty finally something everyone can afford.

Do without and out of debt.

Big shot on pay day and little shot all other days.

The trouble with being broke is that I can't afford it.

Money makes the world go around, and then the day the earth stood still was the day the stock market crashed.

Devote your life to making money and I will show you a slave for hire.

If you wait for the perfect buy, it will pass you buy (by).

I don't have any stocks in any business, and if the stock market falls, it's none of my business.

I give anyone credit for never having credit.

Have a lot, spend a lot, have none, spend none.

I don't have any money to burn, and tax's are like a fire, the more you feed it the more it consumes.

Paradox; Everyday a billion new dollars are printed and we go a billion dollars more in debt.

Debt- Live for today and have no tomorrow.

Debt is due to desire, and I desire to stay out of debt.

If you open a business without a college education, and you lose money, the money you have lost is your education.

A penny earned is a penny saved, and you can bank on that.

A $1,000.00 in the pocket is often worth more than a $2,000.00 I.O.U.

In general the more money you make the less work you do.

If you master money you master greed.

There's plenty of money in this country, and even more in the rest of the world.

I would pay to advertize, but it costs too much says the new businessman.

The cheaper priced an object is the more it may cost.

49% of the people think it is an illusion that money buys happiness, and the other 70% just can't do the math to make money.

Old money spends like new.

I have deficient disorder, see my checking account.

Bullion
Bills   Bullion over bills.

Some people are born with a silver spoon and others are born with chains on.

If everybody were rich the rich would be poor.

Run quickly from get rich quickly.

I'm too broke to be poor.

It takes money to make money, but it doesn't have to be your money.

Gold pays only the interest of a good night's sleep.

The rich not only have someone to wipe their butts, but to kiss them too.

Lonely money multiplies.

Money makes the world go around, and then you find out it's all counterfeit.

Money makes your name Mr.

People want to save money, but they don't want to pay the price.

The change of money is the change of power.

Money is a small slip of paper that many people sell their souls for.

Is there life after death? I don't know, but bury me with a credit card anyway.

No shoes, no shirt, no service, have money, come on in.

Buy low. Sell high, don't cry.

House on fire, but don't call the fire dept, I smoked this house up one cigarette at a time.

Greed only satisfies the poor.

What I need is a new job, what I got was a pay check.

Debt free- one must conserve to preserve.

I wear a blindfold when my wife goes in my billfold.

You have a guarantee and you want your money back, I can guarantee you won't get your money back.

It is far better to loan money to a bank than to a friend.

You can't save your way into heaven, but you can spend your way into hell.

I have what I need and not what I want, so I'm rich.

In life there are two classes, the rich and the want to be rich.

Another day another dollar, then why don't I have any dollars?

There is REST in inteREST.

Dreaming, wishing, and magic, I'd rather have money.

There's a million ways to make a million dollars and you only need one way.

I borrow to pay my bills and now I have no bills, that is so simple any fool can do it.

Many pennies make a million dollars, and so many ways to make a penny.

Old car old headaches, new car new payments.

When keeping up with the joneses you might have to pay through the noses.

Today I work for money so one day my money will work for me.

Budget the pennies.

Money makes you free, and the job to get money makes you a slave.

Penny wise will soon be dollar wise.

You must have patience to learn how to be patient.

The lottery only makes temporary winners.

Las Vegas was built on someone else's money, and I'm one of those many someone else's.

A slow death is debt.

Money- you can't take it with you, but how you got the money may determine which way you go.

The man that said money can't buy happiness was never rich.

At all costs, think before you spend.

The boss pays the cost,
If you are not the boss,
You don't know the cost.

I'm on a strict budget of $20.00 a day unless I spend more today.

If you can't make your mind up you'll make minimum wage up.

Inflation deflates money.

It's better to make a million dollars than inherit 10 million.

The rich help the rich stay rich, and the poor help the poor stay poor.

I am green at making money. (Two meanings to this)

Money flies.

When my money flies I cry.

Credit cards buy now and pay later, and pay later, and pay later.

The only reason I don't have a million dollars is because I have no money.

Unemployment annulled my alimony payment.

Can a man buy his way into heaven? Because he can buy his way into hell!

Paying interest on your credit cards is not in your best interest.

More money, more taxes.

Things made, things bought, more things made more junk bought.

With money in the bank; REST on your inteREST.

Your lack of money is not due to your lack of buying stuff.

When you have no money everything appears on sale.

When a fast talker stops talking and starts walking, check your wallet.

The incentive of being rich is my incentive to get rich.

Money; make it, spend it, make more money, spend more money, buy some discipline.

The dead man finely has enough money.

The buyer- I just gave a fool a rock for some bread,
The seller- Some fool just gave me a hunk of gold for some bread.

Income – outcome = not enough income.

The poor; without them who would be rich?

A job is a form of slavery, money is why we work, but money is a form of slavery; the fact is money gives us freedom.

I make my own poverty, and each year I get better at it.

A penny saved will be taxed later.

Money flies when you buy.

Money talks and shoppers walk.

Those who are rich without money, have more riches than those with money.

Beauty is in the eye of the beholder, and I am beholding some Franklin's, Grant's, and Hamilton's.

No pain no financial gain.

My boss owes me money, I owe the bank money, and my boss gets his money from the bank.

Money has wings.

Buy low, sell high, bye.

I have no money, but I do have my beer and cigarettes.

If you change your life so that you are slow to change your dollars into change, then you will have the change to buy what you need.

I wish I could buy a stock named inflation.

OPTIMIST AND PESSIMIST***********
(Written by Joseph Bonkowski)

Be an optimist when you are down, and it will be easier to get up.

Pessimism makes the will ill.

Optimists look up to heaven, pessimists find a lot of coins.

Things ALWAYS change from bad to worse, and I think it's good to be pessimistic.

Optimists have a pot of gold on the other side of the rainbow; the pessimists doesn't have a pot.

I hope a pessimist will be an optimist, I hope.

Be an optimist first and a pessimist second.

An optimist at youth and a pessimist when older.

That pessimism stuff is all in your head.

A pessimist often falls short.

Pessimist are pest.

POLITICS**************************
(Written by Joseph Bonkowski)

If the people vote in a dictator they won't be able to vote him out.

Politicians are members of the liars club.

You judge a candidate and then vote, you may be asked;" why did you vote for that candidate on judgment day"?

In politics there is the right and the left, I'd rather be right than what is left.

Try to elect a philosopher for president, and if he thinks, he won't run.

A politician's hand fits in many pockets.

There's no room for truth in politics, unless you plan on not being elected.

Politics make for strange bed fellows, the voters.

This is the best group of political candidates ever, and that was the lie that won first place at the liar's club.

Politicians are like magicians what you see is all illusion.

I think they should arrest everyone who is not an independent voter and let the three of us run the country.

Too waste your vote is not voting for the best candidate.

All politicians are going to stop crime, if they meant it they would resign.

To expose truth in politics is to expose a lie.

Election time- Vote for the same crook or a new crook.

Some people steal, but a politician is one you elected to steal.

I vote for the more moral candidate. I don't vote for the more economical candidate. If everyone voted for the economy the economy would fall apart, if everyone voted for the moral candidate things would take care of themselves.

Politicians are like Siamese twins, they both have two faces.

If you want to know where a politician stands ask his opponent.

Most politicians run to line their own pockets, and that's why their hand is in your pocket.

Politicians know everything when it is convenient and know nothing when it is convenient.

To lead most people just tell them what they want to hear, and then do what they want to do.

My congressman is ambidextrous; he can steal money with either hand.

I vote to bring back political hangings, now my politician must put it into a bill.

The only way a bill gets passed is to pass plenty of dollars bills.

If 5 people on the Supreme Court are wrong, it makes the whole nation wrong.

If kickbacks were righteousness, all politicians would be preachers.

Election Day always has two good presidential candidates; the problem is neither candidate will finish in the top two.

A politician will build anything, but you must first build his pockets up.

You can't be too far to the right, but you can be too far to the left, Right?

Bad politicians are re-elected by good people who can't read between the lines.

Which face is the politician talking out of today?

Misquotes wins elections, misquotes lose elections.

The rich pay their tax by the means of a kickback.

To lie, to steal, to mislead, to cheat, too steal some more, it's all politics.

If you vote for the lesser of two evils, you are still voting for evil.

Election time, it could be worse, the candidate you voted for could have won.

Everyone likes a party, democrat or republican, it's all the same, but the real party is the 3rd party.

In politics the right money makes the right wrong and the wrong right.

To change a law takes the changing of money first.

Corrupt politicians are elected by the people who can't read between the lines, but can read a ballet.

Lean to the right or to the left in politics and you will find out most everybody leans the same way.

If you vote for perversion you will vote your way to hell.

Tyrants win by a vote of one to nothing.

Power corrupts, so pull the plug, vote one corruption out and another corruption in.

Freedom costs, tyranny costs more.

Tyranny brings tears to my eyes.

Your voting record won't get you to heaven, but it sure can help you get to hell.

The politician you see ain't the politician you get.

I'm for political in-correction!

One good thing about a member of an ungodly political party is that; that member can still find God.

The thief doesn't call attention to himself unless he's up for re-election.

I rebuke your rebuttal.

A fixed election makes a urinal out of the voting booth.

The act of politics is to act.

A politician must act honest while taking a dishonest kickback.

The best leaders aren't elected, the best politicians are.

Political correctness and liberals walk hand and hand all the way to hell.

Too many idiots vote.

It's not an idiot running it's an idiot voting.

Politics and art are just popularity contests.

Politicians are like magicians, there's always something up their sleeve.

We need honest corruption.

The word change in politics usually means money changes from my pocket to theirs.

The art of politics is to answer a question without answering a question.

Anonymous makes the president.

Power is the person that counts the votes.

If you're willing to vote for the wicked, God may vote you to hell.

Vote for a third party, it's the only way out.

Politicians and magicians, need I say more?

To lie, to cheat, to steal, lets re-elect him.

What this country needs is a good .10 cigar, not a nickel and dime politician.

If a candidate says I promise not to steal as much as the next candidate will, he probably won't get re-elected because everybody knows he will steal more.

In the U.S.A. they have a two party system, and both invite the other to their own parties.

Politicians claim to do what they don't want to, no matter how badly they want to do them.

In politics what your opponent is accusing you of he is doing.

A leopard can't change his spots, so don't elect one.

Politicians and car salesmen what's the difference?

If a politician takes a political party to a place it has never been, then that place should be jail.

The troubles of a two party system are the two parties.

The average politician gets rejected but re-elected.

If a politician were to show his true colors you may not vote for him, most people vote for the more colorful candidate.

Let the republic go public.

Elect enough liberals and they will count their own votes.

The president is much smarter when he reads his speech.

Because 51% of the people voted wrong, they have wronged the other 49%.

The trouble with a two party system is they agree with each other.

I am tired of voting for corruption so I voted for a 3rd party, and when I die I hopefully won't have to explain to God why I voluntarily and knowing voted for corruption!

Politicians and magicians, one makes objects disappear and the other makes money disappear.

You get what you vote for.

I don't pay income tax because I wish to, I pay income tax because you voted that I should, I voted libertarian, and you did not, just because you voted to pay taxes doesn't mean I would like too!!

I think you threw your vote away, and I know you threw our money away!

In politics it's not the four legged rat I fear.

You can't take your words back, but you can be a man of your word.

In most elections if the undecided would vote for a 3rd party, we could have a party.

The president speaks from BrainWashington D.C.

Too many politicians make bad legislation.

New leadership same ship.

An honest politician is not in office.

If you think you can fool 51% of the people run for office.

One man rule is not cool.

If your conduct is unethical you should run for a political office.

(Political) New broom, old dirt.

I have a MAD idea, Alfred E Neuman for president on a write-in ballet.

Politicians pick pockets.

99% of the people don't like to pay taxes, and a third party runs on a platform of no taxes and will get 1% of the vote! WHY?

Stupidity is the act of the average voter.

Bribes are illegal, but contributions are legal.

I would like to be treated like the Company that has donated to a political campaign!

PROCRASTINATIONSEE HABIT******
(Written by Joseph Bonkowski)

I will only procrastinate until tomorrow.

The time for procrastination is now.

Poverty and procrastination are friends.

Willpower will empower.

I have the ambition to procrastinate.

If procrastination were easy everybody would do it.

Procrastination is now or never.

Tomorrow never comes for you; but me, I'll start tomorrow.

I have too much nothing to do.

Everyone finds time for procrastination.

Procrastination today procrastination tomorrow.

Contemplate on procrastination.

Practice makes perfect, so I practice procrastination, and I am almost perfect at it.

I started procrastinating instead of quitting and I won.

I'll do it when I'm through procrastinating.

Procrastination is my habit.

To finish you must start.

Procrastination and failure would walk hand in hand if they could just get off the couch.

I'm doing what I do best and that's nothing.

The only time you have is now.

I can think of 5 good reasons why I haven't done that, and procrastination is not on the list.

It's not procrastination that stops a kid from standing up to a bully.

I like to procrastinate about it before not doing it.

The procrastinator always has an excuse.

The only way you can finish is to start.

The sooner did; the sooner done.

I know I still have not done it, but it's because my will-power is procrastinating.

Do it today instead of tomorrow, for tomorrow you may procrastinate.

Procrastination is a habit that I will break later.

Time does not procrastinate.

Motivation is the kryptonite of procrastination.

Do it today for tomorrow never comes.

Procrastination wears no watch.

If you want something done, give it to a busy man, and I'm too busy watching T.V. to do anything else.

Laziness and procrastination are too complacent to walk hand and hand.

I work hard at getting out of work, so leave me alone I'm working.

The two letter word "do" can kill the 15 letter word procrastination.

A late start is better than an early no start.

I'm still writing my book on procrastination.

There will be plenty of time for procrastination later.

If now is not the time, when is?

Will power is just a lack of procrastination.

Now is the only time you can break procras t i n a t... .. . . . .

If you wait for the perfect time it will never come, unless the perfect time is now.

Death ends procrastination.

I spend my free time procrastinating.

I spend my free time procrastinating and that's why I have free time.

Delay your procrastination and one day there may be nothing to do.

An unread book makes good use of procrastination.

To do or not to do, for that is the question, the answer is to do.

Let me begin anew, but let me begin.

Don't fall into the illusion of later.

No one becomes famous by sitting on their couch.

I have no problems procrastinating.

The wise procrastinate their way out of a fight.

If the best can improve, I know I can, and for now I want to improve my procrastination.

Tomorrow is the day I reserve to do everything.

Procrastination steals your time up to the time of death.

Procrastination has no beginning and no ending.

An ounce of action is worth a ton of procrastination.

If you want something done you have to do it yourself, now wonder why nothing ever gets done, I'm lazy.

The time is now, if not when? Tomorrow may never come, so now is the time.

Fear and procrastination stops success every time.

Now is the only time you can break procrastination.

Procrastination, it's never over.

Do nothing,
Get nothing,
Expect nothing.

I must break my habit of procrastination, and I will start by not procrastinating about watching T.V.

Delay tragedy, delay procrastination.

One day a year has 25 hours in it, I will do everything on that day.

RELIGION****************************
(Written by Joseph Bonkowski)

Warning the following is not scripture!

It's so simple to find God that many people don't.

Rain or shine, they both come from above.

Hell is the punishment to fit the crime, every time.

Can't sleep try church.

Sin I can't help it, I was born that way.

Not every banker has money saved, and not everyone in the church is saved.

Eve put Adam on a fruit DIEt.

The best time to pray is when you don't think you need to.

Only God and a teenager know it all.

Thank God for two, two eyes, ears, arms and legs, thank God for only one mouth.

Christians hang out with Christians, and thieves not only hang out with other thieves but they also hang from trees.

If you play hide and go seek with the devil, it's best not to find him.

When life knocks you on your face, get up on your knees.

A truthful man will say when he dies if he is going up or down, and he will believe it, even if it's a lie.

If you can't find God, you will find hell.

When you get on your knees, your two knees are further from heaven; but, you are closer to heaven.

To steal a man's soul, he must first let you.

God I am willing to do anything for you, but can we start tomorrow?

God gave me wisdom, and with it I know there is a GOD.

My life is a rerun to God.

Can someone explain faith?

Trust in God and make God your trust fund.

Most of the church will meet in hell after death.

Dusty bibles lead to hell.

Looking for a bargain; pray.

It can be easier to find God than a good parking spot.

Don't cross Jesus.

Most of us sing in our cars, but we forget how to sing in a church.

Freedom of religion is praying others will find your religion.

I would give anything to be rich, except a stinking 10%.

Hell is overpopulated, the air conditioning is broken, the water is off, and you volunteer to go there?

There is a big difference between a Saint and Satan.

You believe your way into heaven, you don't believe your way into hell.

I'm not always up but I'm never down.

It's not swell to burn in hell.

There's always time for church, if not there will be plenty of time for hell later.

If you can't sleep go to church.

An almost prayer is still a no prayer.

If you learn from correction you are wise and God is trying to make you wise.

Liberals will try to correct God!

If Elvis is king, then who is Jesus?

Don't worry about what I'm doing; worry about what God wants you to do.

Start the day with a prayer and end the day with a prayer, and the middle of the day might not be so bad.

And The Lord said "let there be light" and Thomas Edison was born.

Don't do as I do, do as the Bible says.

To all of you true Christians reading this, you should be reading your Bible.

Hang out with the devil and you may hang.

Jesus wants everyone saved, does this include the Devil?

Equal pray for equal work.

The bible at dusk is not for growing dust.

Jesus ends with us.

It rained for 40 days and 40 nights, and I didn't have flood insurance.

O great God,
I come before thee,
Not a sinner,
Not with any evil,
Modest in mind,
If you can read my mind,
O what a liar I am.

God is the greatest artist of all time.

All possessions are God's, we just borrow them.

Two world wars didn't bring peace,
Two atomic bombs didn't bring peace,
Only one book can bring peace.

The rich preacher may be teaching and fleecing.

Stand up for God by getting on your knees.

A preacher that doesn't preach about hell may soon visit hell.

A crucifixion is my one way ticket to heaven.

The trouble with taking a lifetime to find God is you never know when your lifetime is up.

Hell is not an overnight stay.

God is my icon.

Many people in hell claim they have done no sin.

Majority hell, minority haven.

The fear of fire put the fear of God in me.

The rich get richer, the poor get poorer, and the evil get eviler.

Can a man run from God?

If you think God is a fool then you are a fool.

The Bible is my book of laws that I obey.

If faith could be seen, we would all believe.

If God is your best friend, then the Bible should be your favorite book.

A seed makes a plant and God makes the seeds.

Some men consider themselves good, and some as god, what a difference an o makes.

Oh- lord my knees hurt, forgive me for not kneeling,
Oh- lord my car is broken, forgive me for not going to church,
Oh- lord my eyes are bad, forgive me for not reading your word,
Oh- lord my bills are due, forgive me for not giving,
Oh- lord forgive me for being an average worshiper!

Hard times require hard praying, good times require hard praying.

Faith- Don't wait to see it to believe it.

From being low or high there is a between, from heaven to hell there is no between.

Look at the bright side you haven't fallen as far as Lucifer.

The poor little sheep that has lost his way, behold, the atheist.

251

A lion is a lion, and a Christian is a Christian, please keep them apart.

The Devil is a rat and God in the cat.

God's plans are better than mine, yet mine are the ones I try to follow.

Sin- starts small big finish.

The wise run to God, the fool runs from God.

The deeper a man sinks in quicksand, the closer to God he gets.

When in doubt pray.

Purgatory is not the waiting room for heaven, but the expressway to hell.

The Bible is the best book that most of us don't read.

The best things after life are free.

Global warming happened at Sodom and Gomorrah.

My plans don't include the devil, but his plans include me.

Don't fall prey to the devil, pray.

Hell has many entrances and no exits.

Prayer is a phone call to God.

Billions eat every day because God is the farmer.

No one can make you believe in God and no one can make you believe in hell.

Do not read the Bible with blinders on.

If you want to make the crippled run, preach to them.

Beware of Satan's counterfeit ways.

Satan and politicians promise you everything and give you nothing.

The deal is God is the only one that heals.

I don't understand for a country based on God, why we vote so ungodly?

I only have one soul, and it practices only to go up.

The biggest difference between God and a judge is God won't take a bribe.

I use biblical duress to keep the devil away.

God is a 24 hour miracle.

I fight my enemies through prayer.

Politically correct is incorrect with God.

Are your political views to the RIGHT or to the LEFT? Let me help you make up your mind, only the RIGHT gate to heaven will open.

Sin to the right of me, sin to the left of me, so what's left? The Bible!

Sometimes God knocks us off our feet so we can start praying.

A new person in God makes a new peace within himself.

If you invest in God over gold, gold may follow.

Idle hands and idiots make idols.

When I get up the first thing I do is put my feet on the floor, the second thing I do is put my knees on the floor.

Pass judgment, I'll see God, not you.

Rule the World and serve in hell.

The thief lets the devil steal his soul.

Hell is too hot for me, but heaven is cool!

God has made today with the hopes you will talk to him today.

Atheist or agnostic your home will soon be hell.

In heaven there is no sin, only good times, so I say to all my enemies drop dead.

I will be reincarnated in heaven.

I freely get on my knees and God freely lets me enter into heaven.

Be fruitful and multiply, so the vegetarian started a course in math.

I thank God that I have time to thank God.

If you think you are smarter than God, then God will soon teach you a lesson.

Have faith in God and God will have faith in you.

Please God and please yourself.

If the rich man is right with money, and the poor man is right with God, I'd rather be the poor man rich with God.

Date of birth,
Date of death,
Do you have a date with God?

A greedy prayer is not heard, a needful prayer is.

If you don't have the time to pray, pray for the time to do so.

The right way,
The wrong way,
Your way,
My way,
And God's way.

Perfect is heaven and perfect is hell, the difference is hell is the perfect punishment, and heaven the perfect reward!!!

I know nothing of God but what God tells me, and God knows all about me, even what I don't tell him.

HELL, no one tells God what to do.

Thank God I'm on my death bed that means the worst is behind me and the best is yet to come.

Many man made Gods can tell many man made lies.

I once had a dream of hell; I now have a search for heaven.

John 3:16 or trade center 911.

Football or church? After football season has ended, the church has the same membership.

We are not guaranteed tomorrow, so that is why I pray today.

I tip less than 10% to God and 15% to my waitress.

Be ever so humble there's no place like heaven.

I would like to write the perfect book, with the sum of all important knowledge, but the bible has already been written.

Lord let there be less of me and more of thee.

Is the soul stored in the heart or the head? From head to sole is the soul stored.

Read the future read revelations.

Do more men die defending religion or die in the name of religion?

Oh- lord help me to see what I am,
Oh- lord help me to see what I am not.

The atheist should pray that there is no God.

God gives the orders, and you don't order God.

To reach the stars climb the stairway to heaven.

We the people are three great words, but three better words are "Trust in God."

Immortality is found while alive.

If you don't believe the Bible you will believe your way out of heaven.

It pays to pray.

To fall from the grace of God is a long long way down.

God has put my enemies over me in my country, and I don't know why everyone keeps voting them back in?

How rich is too rich, when you become rich enough to go to hell.

Ready set God.

If sin is in then heaven is out.

You can't commit suicide in hell.

The fool says there is no God, are you a fool?

If you think heaven is too high to go to, you can be sure hell is too low to go to.

Through the ages God never worked for wages.

Today the church is a show,
Today the preacher is not a teacher,
Today we think we are going to heaven,
Today may be your last day?

My strength is in God, my weakness is in me.

The smart and successful atheist is not so smart and successful, because he did have help from God and Satan.

Read the bible for what it is and not what you want it to be or you will wind up where you don't want to be. (Two meaning to this)

You can't lie your way into heaven.

Do you have doubt in your faith? Or do you put faith in your doubt?

Find God and you've won the lottery.

Your S.S. number is your government given 666.

God- try it you'll like it.

If the devil made you do it, didn't you really want to do it?

Take control of your life by letting God take control of your life.

The best way to stand tall is to be two feet shorter in prayer.

My Bible is my map to Heaven.

Heaven is not about money hell is.

Serve God and God will serve you.

If you fight evil with evil you fight with yourself.

Heaven or hell there's no place like home.

A treasure map with great treasures in it is called the Bible.

There are only two places to go after death, heaven or hell, and if you don't know it, it will be hell!

Psychology was first used by the Serpent on Eve, and then passed from Eve to Adam, etc...

Football or church? God is the score keeper.

Repent for lent.

The Bible has an expiration date, and I don't know that date?

Mankind will never find peace, because he never looks for God.

For many of us the death bed is the only time we think about our souls, but we are not guaranteed a death bed.

If the devil leaves you alone, it's because he has you where he wants you.

Most of the time the devil works overtime and Christians take the day off.

It's best to stand up for God before you lay down in your coffin.

It won't be a great ride if you don't pay the tithe.

There are many saints, and there is only one Satan, thank God.

Satan and Santa Claws both wear red, but Jesus wore it when it counted.

Lord I prayed "I want to be a winner", and it didn't happen, I guess I should have prayed "lord would you make me a winner?"

Judge a man by Gods standard, and if they don't like it, they can take it up with God.

Money first and God second makes for Hell first and hell second.

Nothing is too hard for God, but some things are too hard for my hardhead.

God is with everybody, but not everybody is with God.

There is a big difference between an antichrist and the antichrist.

Most people will do good works right to hell.

Eternity is longer in hell than in heaven.

For the love of God quit loving your money.

For more time in a day, pray one hour a day.

If you bow down to a dictator you will also bow down to The Devil.

The gateway to hell surrounds many churches.

The atheist will be very very hot later; FOREVER!

JESUS is a road seldom CROSSed.

Spend your money in an ungodly manor and you spend your money unwisely.

Hades; how can I get the hell out of there?

Don't bend your morels, instead bend your knees.

The one with the most toys wins, but I found a toy that can give me internal life!

God knows what I am doing, God please forgive me.

We need not pray for what should be common sense; but, sometimes we should pray for common sense.

I am one of one,
I rode a bicycle twice,
And a tricycle three times,
And was a quarter of a quartet on the 4th of July,
I drank a 5th on the 5th of the month,
I shot six shots on my six-shooter on the 6th,
And Thank God I rested on the 7th day.

I'll find God later said the man on his death bed.

Hell is politically correct.

God will make you,
God will break you,
God may even take you.

God is in control, he is like the back seat driver with all of the directions that no one will listen to.

I regret that I have but one God to die for.

God has long arms.

Watch football on a cold Sunday, if this is your life, then next football season might be very very hot.

Do right,
Be right,
Alright.

Most people don't know how to get to heaven, but most of us know how to get to hell.

I may sound like a fool talking to you about God, but to God I sound wise.

Newton saw the apple fall and so did Adam and Eve.

The left is never right when you die.

I would like to go to heaven, but I would like to go tomorrow.

Less government means more God.

I have something God doesn't have, a credit card.

The devil only lies when he talks.

There are no liberals in heaven.

Sin is often the illusion of good.

Better some good, than some evil.

The wicked people think they can tell God the errors of his way.

It's funny how my plans change when they are not God's plans.

The sun is God's light bulb.

I am making real progress when I go from not praying too praying.

Decide on three things in life, God, God, and God.

You can't store both God and vengeance in your heart.

Uncleanness and ungodliness are a set.

A thought about Sunday's, I don't think there will be any football teams in hell.

I can see the future, its heaven or hell?

The hand of God is large enough to handle anything.

God makes your soul grow.

Friend or foe,
Unrighteous or righteous,
Damn or redeemed,
Saint or Satan?

The rich buy the best cars, the best homes, but can't buy a place in heaven.

Look for God, because he's looking for you.

Only a sinner can be saved and we are all sinners.

Comfortable on earth, uncomfortable in hell.

The key to heaven is your bible.

Kill the Christian was shouted for thousands of years, and the Christians are still here, and if you can't beat them join them.

Money can weigh enough to drag you to hell.

If you don't see prayer work- wait.

To pray in good times helps us to keep the good times.

I pray before I eat and I have never starved.

You can't pray your way out of hell.

The people that walk in the light are righteous, the people who walk in the dark are evil, and there may be some gray areas in this statement.

God's ear is attracted to your knees.

God sends us signs and we act as if we can't read.

If you call on God then you should know how to listen to him!

Only eternity lasts forever.

The oldest book in my house is the bible; the newest book in my house is the bible.

Satan holds no copyright on vengeance, God does.

God brings dark night so he can show you his bright light.

Surrender to God and be free.

One minute to pray pays.

Follow the wrong preacher and you follow him to hell.

Religion is on the average 8 hours of T.V. and 8 seconds for God.

A Saint that is made by man just wins the votes.

If God is in control then how do we have free will??

You're famous when you are known after the second coming.

If you plot evil you plot your way to hell.

Plan well and plan Godly.

Thunder is Gods voice saying remember the ark!

I pray that not all prayer be answered.

There is room for you in heaven and also in hell.

A tragedy in life is to have idle hands, but if you build a false idle, you would be better off with idle hands

Rich or poor, fat or thin, old or young, in the end all that matters is where you right and righteous?

When evil surrounds you, turn to God, and let God surround you.

My tithes are my sacrifice at the altar.

Cain caned Abel until Abel was unable to move.

Church- pay, obey and pray.

The devil doesn't rest on Sundays.

When you look for God make sure you don't trip over the devil.

Prey (pray) is food to the Godly.

The bible and money both are made of paper; do you know which is the more valuable?

When Armageddon gets here I hope I'm too old to be drafted.

Immortality; ask God.

I hope to love God as much as God loves me.

The devil discourages, and God encourages.

Guys, God will show you the way, but first you have to ask for directions.

I will follow my God to death, so that I may live forever.

Mankind is smart enough to kill mankind, and stupid enough to try to replace God with mankind.

Hell has no holidays.

You can't find salvation in the Salvation Army, only in God's army.

Take church home, don't stay home.

Hot heads fill hell.

"What harm can one apple do" Eve asked?

Father, Son and holly ghost, against the devil, that's 3 to 1, play the odds.

I was born into sin and maybe that's why I drink gin?

Long live the king, eternal life is long enough.

— — —Sunday Trinity— — —
300,000 at the amusement park,
30,000 at the game,
30 at the church.

A trip to heaven is booked while alive.

God is my travel agent, and I just booked a trip to heaven.

In a crisis ask Christ.

My will is not stronger than God's, but my head is harder than his.

The Bible is my crystal ball.

Some women pray to change a man, a-men.

If you find God you will never find death.

God is my judge, I will try to obey my judge, I am guilty, but the charges will be dismissed because of repentance, and salvation will be the sentence.

God is supreme and not the Supreme Court!

Oh why didn't I find God while alive? Because the devil made me do it!

Man rules, or God rules, one of them is only deceiving himself.

I see God everywhere and the atheist sees him nowhere.

You won't believe the Bible if you only believe every other page.

You can't take ill-gotten gains to hell.

If the loud mouth could do just half of what he says he could do he would seem God like, until God shuts his mouth.

Eve picked apples and Adam had an Adams apple.

My prayer is a phone call to God.

Satan and Santa both wear red all the time, and Christ only once.

If you don't pray God will soon give you something to pray about.

Thank God for the stars and for The Son.

Everybody needs a soul mate, how lucky I am to have two, my wife and God above.

I never did learn to listen, so my prayers seem unanswered.

Global warming will only happen in hell.

A fool walks; a wise man bows his knees and then walks.

Revenge, if God used it, we would all go to hell.

How important is a teacher?
How important is a preacher?
How important is a preacher that teaches?

Revenge is something God does so much better than I could.

On judgment day you will not only be judged for what you did, but what you did not do.

God does not send you to hell, you send yourself!

A little sin goes a long way.

You won't find God with blinders on.

It's hard to preach when you stay home.

My best offence and my best defense is prayer.

God has written the greatest book ever, and that's one for the books.

Advice on how to go to hell, run from Jesus!

The lord give-it and the lord take-it, so I give it so he won't have to take it.

God gave us the sun for a present; God gave us The Son for a present.

Peter built his house upon a rock.

Tithes are the gift that keeps giving.

I read a book on ancient history, it is called the Bible.

Read the Bible literally, and read the newspaper between the lines.

On judgment day Jesus will be my defense attorney.

Evil people rub off.

O' happy belated birthday,
She is so beautiful,
May she live forever,
She has both brass and grass,
She's only sixty centuries old.   (The earth)

The Bible is my paperwork.

Reincarnation is from man to soul.

Run to God; not from God.

Yield to God what is God's and everything is God's.

Heaven is on my prayer list.

Try to please the devil today and the devil will punish you later.

The only ghost that I believe in is the Holy Ghost.

The long arm of the Lord.

Water, ice, steam / God, Jesus, Holy Ghost.

Sin costs more than you think.

The God Damned Supreme Court Has Overturned GOD!!!

If you kill in the name of God, I hope you are willing to die in the name of God?

If you stand up for God and they put you in jail you did not fail.

God is the smartest being in heaven, and that's one reason why there are no liberals in heaven.

If you think God can make a mistake, you're mistaken.

It's not the weak man that falls to his knees, but the wise man.

You can win tomorrow by a prayer today.

Lord knows there's only one good book.

If you try to take God out of history, you will soon be history.

A weapon of mass destruction is to burn a Bible.

All of the armies of the world can't take my soul.

The cross can go higher than any airplane.

The wicked bow willingly before great men, and not willingly before a great God.

No matter how dark things get, let your light shine and never be afraid of the dark.

A man with a bent knee seldom bangs his head.

The devil has one butt and I have two feet, I'm not afraid.

Sin comes in small packages.

There's always room for one more in heaven or hell.

Rare is the atheist on his death bed.

Hell is full of many church goers.

The bible is my text book.

God is all around us,
So we are surrounded,
Surrender and ender,
Or run and rot.

If you hold a grudge God may hold a grudge against you.

Only in your mind is the thought that God can't forgive you.

Hell is full of sinners, and heaven is full of forgiven sinners.

If you take God out of the church and schools the devil will slip in.

Up or down,
Right or wrong,
Heaven or hell?

A well read bible is the elevator to heaven, and an unread bible is the elevator to hell.

God can forgive anybody for anything, but only while you're alive.

The atheist does not believe in fairy tales or God, heaven or hell, but after his death he will believe in hell!

When you except perversion you will also except hell!

Give evil and inch and get a mile closer to hell.

I believe in God today, and the atheist will later.

You might not find God if you agree with sin.

The devil knocks on your door in both good times and in bad times, and it's if you let him in or not that counts!

You need a light to see in the dark, and this is true with salvation.

If you have no food, have faith.

There is no goal to set higher than to get to heaven.

Burn a bible and burn in hell.

For all of you hell raisers out there, there is a place for you called hell.

I try not to judge man by my standards, but by the standards of God, for these are the standards that everyone will be judged by.

The devil is a liberal.

The cross is the wooden ladder to heaven.

I don't approve of bloodshed, except for Jesus to save us all.

Which is true, Satan crossed Jesus or Jesus crossed Satan?

The three forbidden things are not accepting Jesus, not accepting Jesus, and not accepting Jesus.

Jesus crossed Satan.

God observes us, but do we observe God?

VERY IMPORTANT JOHN 3:1 to 3:7

SOCIALISM***************************
(Written by Joseph Bonkowski)

Socialism is 1% rich and 99% poor.

Socialism doesn't work, but social workers do.

Socialism, why work, why eat?

Socialism takes capital, and Capitalism makes capital.

Socialism and unemployment walk hand and hand.

If you're a socialist it is now your turn to work.

BEWARE; the government is handing out free checks.

Socialism; no rights, no money, no food, and no good.

Socialism, we already have welfare.

Socialism doesn't work because there is no work.

Socialism soon makes the money printed not worth the paper it is printed on.

Socialism is when the whole nation is on welfare.

If you are a socialist it is never your turn to work?

The lord said "The pour we have with us always", but the lord is not a socialist.

Socialism is true equality, no one will have anything.

If I wanted socialism, I'd have tithed 90%.

Socialism is when everybody has noting.

I'm not a thief, I'm just practicing socialism.

Socialism is the leech of the country.

Socialism is a 100% discount on everything, but there is no everything!

If you want to lose weight let socialism kick in.

If you want to believe a lie, believe in socialism.

Socialism is the great equality of poverty.

Socialism is too many handouts and not enough hands to hand out.

Socialism goes from the house, to the poor house, to the dog house.

Nobody likes a thief, but for some odd reason many people like socialism?

Robin Hood was a Socialist.

The trouble with a handout is once you give a handout everyone has their hand out.

Socialism, nothing owned, nothing stolen.

Charity begins at home, so I wait for my welfare check.

The bigger the government the bigger the hand out, until the government gets so big everyone needs a handout and then the government also will need a handout.

It is revolting to me not to revolt against socialism.

SUCCESS***************************
(Written by Joseph Bonkowski)

You try or you cry?

There's enough mediocrity for everybody.

If you want to be successful take your own advice.

I must have tried 20 times for success, only 80 more times to go.

Your rewards for success are everything you desire.

Many times good things come from good planning, and bad things come from no planning.

Success comes not from chance, but by enduring the failures.

I lucked into my success; I worked 14 hours a day for over 30 years.

I must confess to be a success is to try not cry, but to try, try, try.

When opportunity knocks, the ability to hear it is rare.

Climb the ladder of success, but watch out for you pulling you down.

Many of us are angry at undeserved success, because we just didn't know that their success was deserved.

Destiny is better planned than stumbled upon.

Sometimes success is made up by the teller of the story.

Success is doing 10% of what we think about.

Success is something we see the end results of, and it usually started with the same start that the person who failed had.

I would be a success if I just didn't get in my own way.

You can only be a success when you are satisfied.

Success, it's where you go or don't go after death.

It is rare when someone does their best, and it's common to say I did my best.

Millions of opportunities known, millions missed, and you need only one.

Success was a ruined man many times.

Success, what's left isn't.

Success is money, good friends, and good friends with money.

The poor stay poor because welfare pays too well.

No good or bad plans have ever worked, it is your actions toward the plans that may or may not work.

Success is a plan of action that you need to act on.

You are the master of your destiny, so why are you sitting there?

You have the same rights to try for success as I do; the right to play the lottery.

I will try to do anything, because in my mind I can do anything.

As coal will turn into a diamond, so will trying turn into success.

Do your best and be a success, do your second best and fail like the rest.

Success comes to those who wait, what are you waiting for?

Success is stress.

The formula for success; eat, drink and inherit.

Success is just a different way of not looking at failure.

90% of success is on you and the other 30% is on how well you are educated.

Success = planning + trying + re-planning and retrying.

To be a success means that you are too busy to make an excuse.

Success = perseverance + planning.

If you think success is for other people it is.

Success is only 1% luck.

IF is the great success stopper.

Success means I'm not a worker or a boss.

When opportunity knocks it is sometimes best to slip the doorman a few dollars.

If you think you got the world by the balls, think again, she's a female.

It's sometimes best if you knock on opportunities door.

The recipe for success is to take all your advantages and use them.

Success is half of life, and trying to get success is the other half.

The best are above the rest, to get to the best you get little rest.

Find God and that is the best success.

I have many more wishes then opportunities, I just wish I had more opportunities then wishes.

Success requires work, hard work, planning, luck and a good night's sleep, the latter I have.

Success is 50% trying and 50% trying.

If you copy the rest you will never be the best.

Success is to fight with all your might.

If you learn from a mistake it's an education and success is an education.

The only success that lasts forever is to find God.

Success is often a little trying and a lot of lying.

Success, aim high, because the bullet will drop, and you'll be on target.

The real power is to take action.

To win comes once in many tries.

Opportunity knocks even to a deaf man, it's just who hears it.

The leaders lead, and the followers play follow the leader.

If you want to know the secret of success; then ask someone, if they tell you, then you know they may be a successful liar.

I never gave up at giving up.

One secret to success is prayer.

The secret to success is plan first, act second, fail third, and repeat until step 3 is missing.

Success in life is what you think it is, and I think it's as simple as that.

A successful plan makes for a successful future.

Do the best you can today, and tomorrow will take care of itself.

If it's not your fault you're not a success, then you have deceived yourself.

You can always do better, you can always do worse.

To live your dreams starts with less sleep.

A penalty for success is to be promoted to a job you hate.

The high price of success is adding on a third floor.

If you do your best, you won't be like the rest.

Success is not just the many times you try, but also how hard you try.

When opportunity knocks don't tell it to come back on the commercial.

Easy said; hard done.

Success is the reward, failure is the punishment.

Success is all about the many hands dealt to you, and how the hands are played.

The only thing stopping me from success is me.

I can dream I am a success, but until I get up and start it's just a dream.

Success is like a headache, and you don't miss a headache that you never had.

A winner is the man that is still happy after finishing last.

One key to success is knowing there are many keys to success.

I set a goal so high I had to fail, and at the bottom of my fall I was still on top.

You don't know how far you can go until you try, but you will know how far you didn't go if you don't try.

TAXES************************************
(Written by Joseph Bonkowski)

Charity begins on pay day.

Death and taxes are a sure thing, but I'm not dying to pay my taxes.

Taxes are nothing but a game of pick pocket.

Well or ill, friend or foe, you have to pay your taxes.

To lower your taxes means voting for a third party.

I will party when a third party gets in.

Poverty it's not just for the poor anymore, it's also for the tax cheat.

The sucker is the taxpayer.

I never voted for a tax in my life, and I get tax extortion every payday.

I cried when I came into this world, and I cry every payday.

Taxes are the perfect crime.

The more I make,
The more they take,
The more I hide,
The more I slide.

The tax man is just a paid bully.

The tax man, the con man, I don't see the difference.

The largest business in the world is collecting U.S. tax dollars.

Cut out the middle man and it will save you money, and as the tax payer I am the middle man.

If you master your destiny, you will find out there is a destiny tax.

Taxes are like hemorrhoids, the pain just doesn't go away.

Taxes are like hemorrhoids need I say more.

I donate to charities, I pay taxes.

The best things in life are tax free.

Slogan for H & R Block, Uncle Sam wants you.

Off with their heads, but make sure their taxes are paid first.

The buck stops here; says the tax man.

If it doesn't raise your taxes the tax payer still pays for it.

The perfect weather is sunny and 70 with no taxes.

If I am free, then you are free, free to pay our taxes.

The rich man says to the poor man "I bet I don't pay more taxes than you." the poor man says I don't pay taxes, and the rich man says "I also don't pay taxes, and that is why I'm rich."

Am I my brother's keeper? My tax dollars say I am.

I have freedom, the freedom to pay taxes whether I want to or not.

The grave robber comes and steals after you are dead, and his name is the tax man.

If the money I paid in taxes were a tax deduction, I'd have more money that could be taxed.

I have not yet begun to fight, unless there's a fight tax.

Equal rights are everyone having the right to a tax audit.

Do the math, more taxes plus more over spending, equals re-election.

To tax and spend freely, now, means they need more tax money later.

Bribes and kickbacks are tax free, and this country runs off of tax free.

God wants 10% and the government wants 40%.

Taxes take a bigger bite than a crocodile.

Mercy is given to me once a year, in the form of an income tax refund.

Free enterprise is not tax free.

The people are taxed,
The land is taxed,
The goods are taxed,
Business passes their taxes on to us,
It's a good thing that money isn't worth much today.

I'm against war, my government spends my tax money on war, yet I am not against my government.

I'd rather be scared into heaven than not worry my way into hell.

Money talks and taxes walk.

Layaway, it's what my paycheck is to taxes.

I am not responsible for the government overspending, so quit over taxing me.

If a tax is not lawful it's awful.

The pot of gold at the end of the rainbow is taxed at 60%.

Birds sing all day long, maybe that's because there's no tax on worms.

Good VS evil, optimist VS pessimism, pay VS taxes.

Between taxes, living and taxes I have spent my fortune.

The government passes change and takes dollars.

When you vote for a political party that will charge you income tax, and you don't wish to pay income tax, you not only throw your vote and your money away, you also help to throw my vote and my money away!

The government pays fetch with my tax money, the government throws my tax money away and I keep bringing it back.

Usury laws do not apply to income tax.

The British are coming, let's tax them.

I voted down new taxes, and they still get passed, does my vote count? About as much as my taxes do.

The insane asylum- what's so insane about not paying taxes?

Another day another dollar, that's .70cents after taxes.

Ask not what your country can do for you; ask how much tax will this country take from you?

The death (Estate) tax is one I would not like to pay. EVER!

What do I buy at a parking meter? What do I buy when I pay sales tax? What do I buy when I park in a parking garage? What do I buy when I pay taxes? I buy the right to say good-bye (BUY) to my money.

Tax man don't lien on me.

I am taxed my whole life, I am even taxed at death, I am taxed to death.

Freedom for all, taxes for all.

Taxes are up and kickbacks are up.

Taxation without representation, I see it every two weeks (Payday).

Something for nothing seems impossible, nothing for something see my taxes.

You are born, you die, and taxed in the middle.

Taxation without representation, don't worry the government will represent you.

If you value money over your freedoms make sure the money is tax free.

I spend my pay check foolishly, and the government spends there part foolishly.

Something for nothing, my tax dollars, and nothing for something, my tax dollars.

Value for your dollar a great idea, value for your tax dollars impossible.

Finder's keepers, tax free.

Inflation is like an alligator, it eats my money up, and the alligator tax takes the rest.

The tax collector has a large profit margin.

Taxes make death seem better.

I guess I do need a psychiatrist, I'm a tax payer.

Too much money then taxes is the answer, too much taxes and money is the answer.

The punk gives his money up, and I am a tax punk.

Death and taxes, I wish death would go ahead and kill taxes.

Taxes are like a bully, if you give once, you are expected to give all the time.

Taxes have teeth.

Taxation without representation, revolution is the solution.

The government claims to take a fair tax without my consent, is that fair?

A good slogan for the income tax dept is "THE BUCK STOPS HERE".

I'll throw my two cents in, and Uncle Sam will take one of them.

I'm not a crime fighter because I let the government take taxes.

You get out of life what you put into it, minus taxes.

This is a spend and tax and spend and tax nation.

I don't think I should pay taxes on money that I have honestly stolen.

The taxes I pay go towards funding a corrupt government, I'm glad my kickback money is tax free.

The tax payers are like bees, instead of honey we give money, and the government is the queen bee.

I cheat honestly on my taxes.

I am very charitable with my tax dollars.

Minimum wage makes minimum taxes due, and millions made by a few and no taxes due.

Remember even your enemy pays taxes.

Taxes are like insurance, you pay for it and you don't use it.

Taxes are like taking candy from a baby, all you can do is cry.

I can do two things at the same time, work and pay taxes.

Taxation without reputation. (Re-read)

The national debt, just print more money.

Every politician claims to lower your taxes at election time, and then elects to raise them.

There is nothing in the constitution that says I have to pay income tax, so please quit voting in the parties that act unconstitutionally.

Taxes are the straw that broke my back.

I pay a lot in taxes and I get nothing, something for nothing.

My tax dollars pay for war and I would like to declare war on the department of taxation.

I never met a tax I liked.

Give and take, I give my taxes and they take my taxes.

If the unemployed voted for taxes, then let them pay them.

As a caterpillar is to a butterfly, so is my money to taxes.

"Open sesame!" said the government to my paycheck.

Brother can you spare a tax free dime?

The American dream is to be tax free.

What can I do for my country? Pay my taxes, what can my country do for me? Let me pay taxes.

Businesses are taxed, the business passes this tax to us by raising prices, it's a good thing money isn't worth much.

Taxes eat more than I do.

The tax bully shows up every payday.

WAR- PEACE **SEE GUNS************
(Written by Joseph Bonkowski)

No money, no war.

War is often a tag team event.

A time for negotiations, and a time to fight, the difference might be the time of negotiations?

Blood is the red ink of war.

Both black and white fight in a war, and then come home to fight until black and blue.

War is money and money is war.

You can't buy a good war anymore.

Two or more make a war.

If you worry about war you are at war already.

In World War I the Kaiser was on a roll.

Peace starves the economy, and war kills my appetite.

Two men fight and three or more make a war.

War is manmade.

What army can stop a nation from falling from within?

War is it worth fighting for?

War is just another name for population control.

The best kind of war is one that never happens.

The reward for peace is another war.

War it doesn't matter who's fighting, but who will pay for it.

Make peace with God before you make war.

Many wars are planned by both sides.

When the government wants war and the people do not, plan on a war.

The love of war makes widows.

The Gulf war, I say let them play golf.

Peace it comes with a price, a price you can't afford not to pay.

War takes many people to hell before their time.

Make love not war, even if it's war you love.

War is what makes peace possible.

War breaks many countries,
War makes many countries.

To win a war is to win the last battle.

To keep the peace we must start a war.

War and doctors, the graveyards are full of the results.

An army costs money, and it may cost more not to have one.

The worst war is the war within.

The government tells us that war is fought for freedom, but they never tell us how much they profit from that freedom.

After war peace is made, after peace war is made.

War or peace? The economy says war, so off to war we go.

If you don't work hard at peace, you will work harder in a war.

If you make peace because you are not strong, you will not hold up under the weight of peace.

If the cold war is over, then why do we still sell cold medicine?

One man can't fight a war, but one man can start one.

Most of the time it is not the actions of the war that wins the war, but the organization of the actions.

Peace is best organized by organizing a large army.

In chess the game is over when you capture the king, in war the game is over when you capture the king's money.

War, if we need one the government will give us one.

Nonviolence is the weapon that doesn't kill.

Money makes both war and peace.

War is a sign of weakness and a sign of strength.

Often a country can't afford to win a war.

War after war, year after year, war after war, year after year, war after war, it's monotonous.

Stop fighting and start the war.

The worst war any country can fight is from within.

In war both sides pray to God and only the winner tells the story of God's glory.

World war III will be fought with hundred dollar bills.

War doesn't look so bad when sitting at home.

WISDOM*************************
(Written by Joseph Bonkowski)

Happiness over wealth is a sign of wisdom.

A wealth of wisdom comes from being knocked down many times.

The day the wise man stops being asked questions, is the day the wise man should check to see if he has become a fool.

Now wise, once a fool.

I have learned that to learn something once, it may be used a million times or just that one time.

If you never give advice, you will never give bad advice.

Experience
Inexperience   Experience over inexperience.

Most of the many many books that you have read do not interest me, and the book that I have read interest you not.

Judge not yourself wise, let others do this, and if you do this you become wiser.

Uneducated people can read a book; they choose not to because that is part of being uneducated.

Beauty can change the mind of wisdom.

Wisdom is measured partly by how long it takes to admit you made a mistake and the fool by how long it doesn't take.

You can't see wisdom, but everyone can see if you have it.

The wise man will recheck his side of the argument just to make sure he is still the wise one.

Wisdom is nothing but many ignorance's that we have learned from and endured.

Almost every book is a key of knowledge; don't use your key to lock the library.

Wiser words were never spoken than by the man who said nothing, but took action.

Genius is learned fast, wisdom is learned slowly.

A wise man does not go around boasting of his knowledge, but a fool does.

Genius is book smart, wisdom is life smart.

Thought is developed in the darkroom of one's mind waiting for the light to go on.

A wise man thinks about as much as a fool speaks.

The result of a good education is knowing how dumb you were before.

Use your time wisely, use your money wisely, use your experience wisely, and you use your life wisely, wisely said.

Knowledge is king, so volunteer to be king.

The words never spoken are sometimes the best.

The wise man knows that silence is golden, and I could just listen to him all day long.

Philosophy is common sense made common.

To the person that knows all the answers, do you also know all the questions?

The wise man tries to see all options, and then he takes his best options, the fool takes the first option.

Take my advice, no matter how many times you give it, it's never missing.

A search for wisdom can only be found in one's mind.

I was so smart I was stupid.

Philosophy- I always did like short stories.

I'd rather think than study.

We are what we think.

I know a man by his words or lack of words. (Two meanings)

Everything is made up of atoms, neutrons, God and electrons.

Sometimes you can be so smart that you outsmart yourself.

It is good to be wise, and it is good to be rich, it is better to be wise and rich.

To learn something once is to know it for life, this seems like such a bargain that I don't know why we all don't try to become know it all's.

To think, to learn, to study, it still won't make you smarter than the know it all.

Think twice act once.

The book of knowledge is called my Bible.

Part of wisdom is to share wisdom.

Knowledge is number one, and number two is to hire someone with knowledge.

Lend a man your ear, but not your money.

Learning is just something simple that you did not learn yet.

College takes 4 to 8 years and a lifetime to unlearn what you have learned.

The wise man wasn't born wise he learned it, but the fool may just have been born a fool.

The wise man knows 1% of all knowledge, and the fool knows the other 99%.

It's not that I am so smart; it's that everyone else is so dumb.

Ignorance makes for one long argument.

The wise walk while the fool talks.

Conversation is showing off ones education, or ones lack of education?

Hard study today is easy knowledge tomorrow.

WHY?

A brave man fights man to man, a wise man fights with ink.

Time can't have wisdom, but without time we can have no wisdom.

A genius learns from a book, someone with wisdom learns from life.

He who has been there gives good advice.

A blind man can see a wise man.

Books are the key to knowledge, try to become a locksmith.

Even a know it all can learn.

Brain power weighs more than a dumbbell.

I pray for wisdom on my knees, and when I get wisdom, it usually knocks me to my knees.

The parent teaches the child, and sometimes the child teaches the parent.

Wisdom
War.   Wisdom over war.

The wise let go of anything dragging them down.

Wisdom knows what fertilizer is and what it is not.

It is the wise man that asks the foolish question.

Some of the wisest words ever said are "I don't know".

All knowledge is easy after you know it.

It takes your consent to make you study or stupid.

Give someone knowledge and you will get knowledge back, this is known as the law of intelligent conversation.

The wise man talks and listens, the fool just talks.

The older I get the more I find out what I don't know, and the more I don't care about not knowing.

Wisdom doesn't assure success, but if you have the wisdom to be happy, then you will find out that you are a success.

Knowledge is a gift to the mind, and gifts somehow keep giving.

The wise man never tells anyone he is smarter than they are.

Wisdom is to let the brain retain.

When the tongue gets its own brain is this the start of wisdom or of becoming a fool?

You can't force someone to know anything, you know.

The wise man seeks and the fool speaks.

Wisdom knows the time for silence.

If you do what I do you are a fool, if you listen to me you are a genius.

Wit can be humor, half wit can be humorous.

I am sad to say today,
That I can't spell very well,
So I tell it to the teacher,
So I tell it to the preacher,
I have a study buddy,
Why cry when I can try,
I will not give up the fight,
The end is in my sight,
I write until I'm right,
And some day I will be able,
To tell how well I spell.

When I was a kid study was like work, so I tried to study less, now as an adult I must work more because I did not study.

College teaches ideas that only wisdom can correct.

The third time is the charm, the first two times are practice.

I know that I don't know what I don't know, and I know that I know what I know.

There is a large difference between education and common sense.

What is wit, but smart from a side view.

The wise man never thinks he's too smart, I think that's what makes him wise.

Intelligence is picking out a good part of what you have learned and keeping it, and knowing the rest is false.

Speak with wisdom, it echoes.

Don't neglect your intellect.

Being wise I said nothing, or was it from being dumb I said nothing?

To study in any field makes you smarter in many fields.

If you don't want to learn it, you won't.

Don't become so smart that you become dumb.

Knowledge is the encyclopedia of the mind.

Wisdom comes from life and learning, but a fool comes with no instructions.

If old age were wisdom, then the old folk's home would be the collage.

Wisdom makes the mind grow large and still keeps your hat the same size.

Education and common sense are two different things; your common sense should tell you this.

Don't ever let your head get so swollen that your halo won't fit.

Education is the key and your mind is the lock.

I am king said the crazy man out loud, I am king thought the wise man.

Saying "I was wrong" comes with wisdom, and not by always being right.

Wisdom deceives the fool.

The smartest man doesn't know it, for he knows how much he doesn't know.

The trouble with wisdom is you usually have to get knocked down to get it.

Your mind is like a light bulb, sometimes it's dim, sometimes it's burnt out, sometimes it's bright, and sometimes we need to change it.
If you don't think you can think, think again.

Sometimes wisdom is just as simple as moving out of the way of trouble.

To know or not to know, a book is the answer.

If you think that you are wise, study all of the dumb things you have done, if you still think you're wise, I'll show you a wise fool.

Philosophy is nothing more than writing down one's pursuit of wisdom.

Anyone can have an idea, that's what I think.

Idiots ignore ideas and wit works with wisdom.

If you want to know, you must grow.

Too ask takes but one minute, to ask not can take a lifetime.

The wise man asks.

Share your knowledge and more will come back.

The search for knowledge and the finding of it is the result that comes from that search.

Wisdom comes with age and yet there's still the old fool.

Education is both learning and unlearning.

No one can teach me what I don't want to learn.

All of the knowledge in the world is not worth much if you don't use it.

I am a literary genius, and a technical illiterate.

The man that is too smart to share his knowledge has not knowledge enough to share.

Timing is everything, especially when you open your mouth.

Wise and young is rare, wise and old is rare.

I'd rather be a smart guy than a wise guy.

Wisdom it's what philosophy is about.

True wisdom is learning the lesson before the mistake.

When a genius is wrong, he just changes the equation.

Knowledge can be learned later, and I have a lot of later in me.

Knowledge is held in the attic of your mind.

Knowledge is held in the filing cabinets in your mind.

Knowledge echoes.

The fool and wise man might have the same hat size.

Too much education makes you a wise guy.

Knowledge brings knowledge.

The wise man that talks to another wise man need not mention how smart he is, but the fool speaking to the wise man must.

WRITING*************************
(Written by Joseph Bonkowski)

Half the people can't read properly, so I shall sell my book to the other half, the half wits.

Enough good literature can move a book shelf.

To be correct is how the press prints it.

Don't believe what others have written about you, and especially what you have written about yourself.

Write about what you know even if it blows.

I think before I write a book that I should actually read one.

I wrote a book, it should sell well because there's a sucker born every minute, how many suckers can I sell one to?

I don't like anything I ever read, so now I write, and now I don't like anything that I have written.

If you re-write something too many times, does it ever get written?

One good page of writing is seven O.K. pages in the trash can.

I almost finished writing a book, all I have to do is put it down on paper.

Have an idea; write it down, so it is written, so it is done.

In the books I write no one actually lives, but they do die.

A book is the alcohol of knowledge, drink it up.

This space is   reserved for my writer's block.

The writer must do his homework before his paper work.

Thinking on paper is called writing, how's your writing?

Write your sins on paper and give them to the police and you're arrested, give them to a publisher and it's a book.

If I had time I would write a thicker book, if I had any brains I wouldn't be writing at all.

God is both the prolog and epilogue.

Write about what you know and it won't blow.

Reading makes you think, but thinking doesn't make you read.

Maybe a writer is shy and doesn't like to talk so he writes, after several books I wish he'd shut his big fat book up already.

Is the press a lie on paper or one idiot's opinion?

If I would have known I was going to be a writer I would have learned how to write.

News is often an illusion.

Simple message- simply write,
Complex message- simply write.

A quote is nothing more than a short form of poetry.

Don't judge me by the books I own, judge me by the book I read.

Words can be sharper then a knife.

Words of a feather flock together.

A writer writes for your imagination not his.

Philosophy; some are real thinkers and some are real stinkers.

A writer's mistake is often the best part of the story.

I'm not a very literate writer, but I just wrote a book, it's not fiction, I just made it up.

Good writing outlives the writer.

A writer just shares his imagination.

I don't know if it's a true story that I just made up? (Two meanings)

My wishful writing may come true, but not true for me, but still I write and wish it were me.

The books you own tell a lot about you, the books you read tell more, and the books you don't read tell even more.

To write is not always right.

A good writer stays alive long after his death.

A good book makes the imagination soar, and a bad book only gets one page read.

To read a book and find an error is proof that you have read it, or proof read it?

If it ain't on a bumper sticker it ain't philosophy.

Words of wisdom can be written down by someone who doesn't know how to write. (Two meanings)

A good book of 200 pages once was 400 pages.

I was once a writer, then I sold a book, and now I'm an author.

The best known authors can hire a ghost writer, and sometimes this is done after he becomes a ghost.

To make nonfiction better, base it on fiction.

Writing is a job that pays even after you die.

A good book is like a friend that you can't wait to see, and it's also more interesting than your friend.

If it's on a bumper sticker it must be worth reading.

Bad writing is just an opinion, good writing is just an opinion, and people buy opinions.

If the rest is still unwritten, and I'm writing this, so this leaves one less thing unwritten.

Thick books are written one word at a time.

Any fool can write something, but can any fool sell it?

To write is just one way communication on paper.

I don't like to read so I became a writer.

I own a library of books for you to ask me about, I can only hope you ask me about the one book that I actually read.

To re-write a lie is to re-tell a lie.

Nonsense sells.

The brain tells the hand what to write, I wish my hand could spell better.

"Them are fightin' words", if I knew what they meant, then we would be fighting.

I thinks there forth I are, I hates grammar, you no.

He who rules writes and re-writes if necessary.

The real power is the power of the press.

A good book turns illusion into reality and reality into illusion.

All of the good writers re-write and re-re-write.

Eye never needeed no schoolling.

Talk is cheap, slander is not.

One nice thing about writing quotes is it's hard for the editor to change them.

Writers block is a way of telling the writer the writing is boring.

The best writing uses simple words put simply.

I've written more books than I read.

Can't read well,
Can't spell well,
Can't write well,
Well my book does sell.

The penalty for writing bad books is that someone might read them.

To be or not to be? For what is the question?

O' how thy brain wish'th it could pen like Shakespeare,
Bless'd with rhyme and reason for all four seasons,
But alas the pen hath ink'th that stink'th,
Thy rhyme not come'th,
Thee reason missed thee season,
'thus time to end this pen on paper.

Shakespeare is the alpha and omega of language'th.

Shakespeare is the king of babble, and the master of language, alas we know him not.

O' how I would like to write like Shakespeare,
With such rhyme and reason that I can't even read it.

O' how I would like to write like Shakespeare,
With such rhyme and reason that no one could read it.

O' how I would like to write like Shakespeare,
With such rhyme and reason that no one could read it,
I know I am there when even I don't know how to read it.

Any quote can be quoted and you can quote me on that.

I never read my obituary.

I read my own writings and they are trash, but trash sells.

Fiction it's our future.

The lies I wrote are between the lines, and so is the truth.

A writer is someone who puts talk down on paper.

Scandal is all what the press makes or doesn't make of a story.

The press will let you know your opinion.

The gossip column and the truth don't mix; I read this in the gossip column.

The rewrite was something dumb written for something better thought.

When punctuating, I think, I use, too many, coma's, period.

Good fiction is based on nonfiction.

Writing speaks.

The novelist writes in one hundred pages what I can write in one.

If writing reads wrong, rewrite it right.

The biographer is just a stenographer.

Why write a novel when a 1,000 page book will do?

Don't tell me you don't like to write, put it in writing.

What I need is not a rewrite, you need a re-read.

If it reads too good to be true, then I wrote it.

I have the capability to write great quotes, I don't have the capability to follow them.

I may write 100 quotes a day, and in 100 days I may write one worth quoting.

Writing is illusion on paper.

Poetry is just a short book that I don't care for.

Second rate authors need a second job.

First rate authors make writing their first job.

Writing is easy when you don't know how and hard when you know how.

The writer writes the truth, the editor turns it into a lie, the people read the lie, and this is what I write.

Good writing is illusion on paper; bad writing is disillusion on paper.

A good book lives forever.

If the press told the truth they would have to tell on themselves.

Intellectual concept creates genius, and I wish I knew what I just wrote.

The ignorant write serious comedy.

To quote me is to gossip about me.

My quotes are just my ideas that I allow you to read.

If ain't ain't a word I ain't going to use it.

The writer writes for money, one ink for another.

When I'm not writing is when I write best.

A true writer is secure in his insecurities.

Write only fine paragraphs and your book will never get finished.

It's not if you can write well, it's if you can write it well.

It's not if you can write well, it's if you can write well. (The first well is handwriting well, the second well is writing sentences well).

Everything ever written is false, including this statement.

How can anything be fiction if it's in someone's head?

The word allegedly, allegedly makes slander O.K.

The autobiography of a liar does not mention the liar part.

Tragedy is life, tragedy is death, and tragedy is what I'm writing.

I can read 10,000 philosophies or one novel, I hope the novel stinks.

I gave up writing so I would have more time to write.

Journalism is one way one man can express his philosophy.

I wouldn't write any book that I wouldn't buy.

I wouldn't write any book that I wouldn't buy, and I'm broke.

Bad writing's bad only when your mother says it is.

If you're mother edits you mouth while small, great words will come out of it when you're tall.

I'd be a philosopher if I could think better, instead I'm a writer.

Everything that has been written or ever will be written is all in the dictionary, and it's just rearranging the words that make for good or bad reading.

I can write until pens are outlawed.

I don't need facts I'm a writer.

To order a copy of this book go to www.xulonpress.com or ask your local book store.

The end comes at the end, the end.

LaVergne, TN USA
15 December 2009
167123LV00001B/2/P